On rare occasions tl [to the]

level of myth. Patrici [ul play]

Eclipsed ... touches tl

Worcester Magazine l

... the play's real the [times,]

grace and listening t [iat we]

should do when things fall apart and the old signposts disappear...Eclipsed is a play with many levels: spiritual, feminist, even Irish too; about dreams gone sour for the unwanted and outcasts, ... not unlike those who gave Christ such a bad name as He consorted with tax collectors, outsiders, losers and adulterous women. Middlesex News Mass. USA 1994

Audiences walk away from Eclipsed with a communal knot in their stomachs – a sour feeling from having seen a piece of Irish history that people rarely talk about and a slice of Irish culture many would rather not remember. ... This is a story about judgement and it is a story about Ireland. But it is for anyone with compassion in their hearts and the conditions of women in their minds.
Southbridge News Mass. USA 1994

Her stage play, Eclipsed, changed everything. A play that was as faithful to the lives of the characters represented as it was to the hidden stories could almost not have had another author.
President Michael D. Higgins.

This 'subversive and devastating play, Eclipsed, won her international recognition as a writer of courage and finely tempered imagination. John O'Donohue author of *Anam Cara.*

Mothers for a moment, then cloistered forever. ... powerful and thought-provoking. The New York Times 1999

Patricia Burke Brogan's historically compelling and vividly staged new Irish drama unearths little known story ... Los Angeles Times

Total Eclipse of the Heart -- a tremendous play -- many people are just overwhelmed by its power.
Colin Lacey, Arts Section, Irish Voice NY 1995

Ms. Brogan paints a canvas filled with vivid portraits that reveal the full tragedy not only of the penitents but of the emotional price paid by their carers and keepers. Elyse Sommer, Curtain Up

Eclipsed contains a great dramatic force, a cry of horror for a life that slips away without a chance of being lived.
Mauro Martinelli of Sipario, Firenze (Translation) 1995

Eclipsed is a celebration of Life, of Freedom, an exaltation of survival at any cost. It is a story of women united, joined by the same pain and sad destiny, women who were strengthened by their tragic experiences. I was struck by its chorality, by the idea of a group which is always on stage -- every character is finely drawn and all roles are really beautiful -- by the fact that it is a play for eight women, very unusual in theatre.
Massimo Stinco, Dottore in Discipline delle Arti, della Musica, dello Spettacolo, Associazione Teatro Firenze

To deal with such a difficult subject requires both the skill and sensitivity of the artist -- Perhaps it is the kind of subject only the artist is really capable of exploring. By dealing with those dark corners of our collective social and historical experience, the dramatist has the chance to bring light, compassion and understanding in a way no one else can quite achieve.
Jeff O'Connell, The Galway Advertiser, February 1992

Shining light: Irish playwright Patricia Burke Brogan rightly won a Fringe First for this excellent new play and deserves praise for bringing the whole issue of the 'penitent women's laundries' to the public eye - an excellent important play.
The List, 1992.

There is a scene in which the women try to comfort the distraught Mandy ... that would make a stone weep with its pathos and sense of the sweetness of life gone to waste. The Guardian, 1992

This is powerful and moving theatre, all the more powerful because it is understated. Evening News, 1992

A compelling Irish play called Eclipsed brims over with darkness and light, rising from Ireland's boggy soil like a wailing banshee ... Ray Loynd, Los Angeles Times, 21 April 1995

A sterling ensemble achievement, alternately scalding and magical in its theatricality. Los Angeles Times April 23 1995

Well written, witty and poignant, Eclipsed unfolds like a young rose, each petal revealing the sad, sad stories of these forgotten women. The Nine Mass. USA 1994

Despite a seemingly bleak and dark subject matter, the play is filled with humour and celebration ... and the script is well-crafted and subtly poetic. This is a fine piece of work and deserves a large audience. Seattle Fringe Review Rag 1995

Eclipsed .. is one of those rare theatrical experiences so profoundly moving that some scenes tear your heart out. Contra Costa Times San Francisco 2004

Patricia Burke Brogan's plays have always seemed a little ahead of their time. The Irish Times 2006

Burke Brogan's Eclipsed rescues Ireland's Magdalene women from the amnesia at the centre of the nation's nativist history.
Although rarely acknowledged as such, Eclipsed first introduced the tropes by which other contemporary retellings have narrativised the Magdalene experience.'
Ireland's Magdalene Laundries and the Nation's Architecture of Containment, James M. Smith 2007

Eclipsed

Patricia Burke Brogan

Wordsonthestreet

First published in 1994 by Salmon Publishing,
Reprinted in 1997, 2001 & 2005

Fifth edition published 2008 by
Wordsonthestreet
Six San Antonio Park, Salthill, Galway, Ireland
Web: www.wordsonthestreet.com
Email: publisher@wordsonthestreet.com

This edition published 2018 by Wordsonthestreet.

Patricia Burke Brogan
'Inisfáil' 42, College Road, Galway, Ireland.
Telephone 353(0)91567684
Email: burkebrogan@eircom.net

A catalogue record for this book is available from the British Library.

ISBN   978-0-9552604-4-5

Cover Design: Wordsonthestreet
Cover etching: Patricia Burke Brogan
Author photograph: Joe Shaughnessy
Layout and typesetting: Wordsonthestreet
Printed and bound in the UK

Acknowledgements

For their advice and support, I wish to thank: Fintan O'Toole, Rebecca Bartlett, Eugene McCabe, John McGahern, Gerald Dawe, Bernard Farrell, John Lynch, The Association of Irish Playwrights, The Tyrone Guthrie Centre, Dermot Duncan, my brother and sisters, my husband and all my friends.

Eclipsed is a work of fiction and any resemblance to people living or dead is purely coincidental.

Eclipsed is registered with The Writers' Guild of America East and associate worldwide Guilds.

In memory of the Magdalenes

Other Plays by Patricia Burke Brogan

Credo   A Monologue
Requiem Of Love   A Monologue
Yours Truly   Two-Act Play
Cell   Radio Play
Ladies' Day   Verse Play
Stained Glass at Samhain   Two-Act Play
Clarenda's Mirror   Two-Act Play

PLAYS FOR CHILDREN
Rehearsal For A Miracle   One-Act Play
Boats Can Fly   One-Act Play

SCREEN PLAYS
Custody Of The Eyes
Seen and Unseen

List of Characters

Brigit Murphy
Cathy McNamara
Nellie-Nora Langan
Mandy Prenderville
Juliet Mannion
Rosa/Caroline
Sister Virginia
Mother Victoria

Eclipsed

| **Location:** | *Interior of Convent-Laundry* |

| **Time:** | *Act 1 Scene 1 and Act 2 Scene 6 are set in 1992. All other scenes are set in 1963.* |

| **Characters:** | **Sister Virginia** *(White-veiled novice)*
Mother Victoria *(Black-veiled Mother Superior)* |

The nuns are dressed in veil-coif-domino-guimpe (armour-like pre-Vatican 2 clothing with large black Rosary beads and long black leather belts).

> **Juliet**: *A seventeen-year old orphan.*
> **Rosa:** *Daughter of Brigit, who has been adopted and raised by a well-to-do American family.*

Penitent Women *(Unmarried mothers)*
> **Cathy**
> **Nellie-Nora**
> **Mandy**
> **Brigit**

The penitents are dressed in shapeless worn-out overalls with white aprons, black laced-up shoes and thick black stockings.

Nellie-Nora *to be aged for* **Act 1 Scene 1** *and for* **Act 2 Scene 6.**

Set

Purple muslin drapes/cobwebs/washing hang from top of set. Centre hanging/drape covers basket downstage, other hanging drapes are spaced at intervals upstage. In **Act 1 Scene 2** the drapes are used as background/cloister for **Morning-Call** in convent and chapel.

At opening of **Act 1 Scene 3** the drapes are pulled away energetically by the women to reveal work-room in laundry. Door up centre leads to corridor with convent/cloister on right and washing-machine area of laundry on left.

Sound

Orchestral introduction to *He was despised* from Handel's Oratorio *Messiah* and part of the contralto aria *He was despised*, sung by Kathleen Ferrier are used in **Act 1 Scene 1** and in **Act 2 Scene 6.**

Plain Chant and Elvis songs may be recorded.

PROLOGUE

Act 1 Scene 1

Time: *1992*
Sound: *Orchestral Introduction to He Was Despised from Handel's Messiah continues with lines sung by Kathleen Ferrier "He was despised. Despised and rejected. Rejected of men."*

(In darkness Nellie-Nora and Rosa come down stairs into dusty, cobwebby basement. Nellie-Nora with dragging-slipper-walk carries torch and a bundle of large keys. Large laundry basket covered with suspended drape down centre. Nellie-Nora, breaks through cobwebs /drapes. Small cupboard with shelves down left. An old St. Brigit's Cross hangs on cupboard. Old radio on top shelf. Nellie-Nora searches for light-switch, puts on light. Music stops. Rosa is dressed in to-day's fashion.)

Nellie-Nora:	You've come such a long distance! From London (Boston, New York, Los Angeles)!
Rosa:	It's not so far, Nellie-Nora! It's only an hour (5 hours) on the plane!
Nellie-Nora:	I hope you find something to help you. I hope you find what you're looking for.
Rosa:	I hope so, Nellie-Nora! When I found her name, Brigit Murphy, and this address in my adoption papers, I had to come!
Nellie-Nora:	Anything that's left from those times is in this basket!

(Rosa moves to basket. Nellie-Nora opens basket. Creaks of old basket. Pause. Nellie-Nora takes out a nun's black habit, holds it up, folds it across her arm. She then takes out Sister Virginia's pinned together white coif-veil-domino, holds it up. Taking habit and veil-coif, she shuffles/fades towards exit, but stays at exit.)

Rosa: Thank you, Nellie-Nora!

(As Nellie-Nora shuffles towards exit, low lighting shows shadowy shapes of Mandy, Brigit, Sister Virginia and Cathy behind drapes. Very shadowy scene. Rosa searches in basket and takes out an old apron, a sheet and mannikin's head. In an old Black Magic chocolate box, she finds black-and-white photographs, examines them, turns one over and reads.)

Rosa: "To Mandy Prenderville with all my love.
Yours forever and ever and ever. Your
Darling, Elvis Aron Garon Presley."

Ghostly women's voices sing one line of Elvis' song.
"Well, since my baby left me"

(Rosa smiles. Turns over another photograph and reads)

Rosa: "Rem. the Carnival in Cillnamona, the
great craic, Brigit!
Yours forever, John-Joe." – Brigit!
"To Brigit from John-Joe." – John-Joe!
Who is he?

Pause. Takes another photograph. Reads.

Rosa: My baby Rosa. My beautiful baby.

(Rosa stares at photograph. Takes a large battered ledger from basket, opens it, flicks through pages, stops, opens other pages, stops. Reads.)

Rosa: Penitent women in Saint Paul's Laundry,
Killmacha, 1963 Dempsey, Mary Kate –
a boy, James. Signed in by her parents, Mr.
and Mrs. Dempsey. O'Donnell, Betty Ann –
a girl, Agnes. Signed in by her parents.
McNamara, Cathy –

Voice of Cathy:

Twin girls, Michele and Emily. Signed in –

Rosa: Langan, Nellie-Nora –

(Rosa turns to Nellie-Nora as Nellie-Nora exits.)

Rosa: Nellie-Nora?

Woman's Voice:

A stillborn boy. Signed in by her employer, Mr. Persse. –

Rosa: Mannion, Julia –

Voice of Juliet:

A girl, Juliet. Signed in –

Rosa: Prenderville, Mandy –

Voice of Mandy:

A boy, premature, stillborn.

Rosa: Murphy, Brigit –

Brigit's Voice: A girl, Rosa.

(Searches and finds baby-photograph in chocolate box.)

Rosa: *(puzzled)* Brigit Murphy – a girl, Rosa? – My Mother! – Penitent?

(Rosa moves to small cupboard down left, searches through shelf, touches St. Brigit's Cross, old radio and, as if following Nellie-Nora, exits through drapes.)

Straight into **Morning Call, Act 1 Scene 2**

Act 1 Scene 2

MORNING CALL

Time: *1963*

Sister Virginia, holding lighted candle, moves between cloister-drapes and rings small handbell.
Sister Virginia: *(Chants)* Benedicamus Domino!
Voice of a nun: *(Chants)* Deo Gratias!

(At each "cell door" Sister Virginia repeats morning call and a voice answers.)

Four Calls.

(Sister Virginia quenches candle and exits through drapes.)

Straight into **Act 1 Scene 3 Cathy's Birthday.**

Act 1 Scene 3

CATHY'S BIRTHDAY

Time: *1963*

Lighting: *Low. Straight from Scene 2 Morning Call. Nellie-Nora, Brigit and Mandy enter energetically through purple drapes. Mandy and Brigit pull down drapes, fold them rhythmically and put them on shelves up right. Colour of drapes contrasts with darkness of walls. Old shop mannikin wearing Bishop's crimson soutane with white surplice folded across shoulder up left. Energy, light!*

Sound: *Women sing* "Heartbreak Hotel" *(Elvis style)*
                    "Well, since my baby left me
                    I found a new place to dwell.
                    Is down at the end of lonely street
                    At Heartbreak Hotel.
                    I'll be so lonely, baby!
                    Well, baby, so lonely!
                    Well, baby, so lonely I could die!"
(Nellie-Nora works at ironing-board down left.)
Mandy: Any sign of him, Nellie-Nora?

(Nellie-Nora runs down centre, and stands on chair, her back to audience. She balances old cracked mirror towards imaginary window as she tries to see the outside world in response to Mandy's query.)
Mandy: *(excitedly)* Is he here yet?

Nellie-Nora: Aahk! The window's too high up, Mandy!
There's no light! The glass is too thick! It's
like the bottom of a jam-jar! This mirror's
cracked too! Shh! – I thought I heard
something! – Maybe it's himself! –
No! – No!

Brigit: *(imitating Mother Victoria's voice)* Whaaat
are you doing, Nellie-Nora? You're a
disgrace! What about His Lordship's linen?

(own voice)

Careful! If you break that mirror, you'll have
seven years bad luck! *(Mandy smiles.)*

Nellie-Nora: Sure I must have broken a lorry-load of
mirrors to end up in this saltmine!

*(Nellie-Nora blesses herself and manipulates mirror again.
Mandy genuflects towards Brigit.)*

Nellie-Nora: No sign of him, Mandy! Maybe he got a
puncture! Ahh! I thought I might see a little
sunshine between the iron bars. Mother
o'God! Back to penance!

*(A convent bell rings. Mandy takes mirror and tries to see the
outside world.)*

Brigit: Never mind that fella, Mandy! Sure you
don't even know his name!

Mandy: He's a smasher, Brigit! Did you never hear
him whistling to me?

(Nellie-Nora searches her pockets.)

Nellie-Nora: Where did I put that butt? A match, Mandy!
A match quick!

Mandy: Here, Nellie-Nora!

*(Nellie-Nora lights cigarette butt and keeps it between her
lips as she speaks.)*

Nellie-Nora: Mmn! That's better!

Mandy: Aah! No sign!

Nellie-Nora: Keep trying, Mandy!

Brigit: Shhhh! She's coming!

(Brigit and Mandy rush to wash-board-basins and pretend to work. Nellie-Nora puts out cigarette, hides it in fold of her short stocking and returns to ironing-board down left. Mother Victoria enters, nose high in the air and stands down centre.)

Mother Victoria:

I hope His Lordship's linen is ready, Brigit! Show me that surplice, Nellie-Nora!

(Nellie-Nora comes forward with surplice. Mother Victoria examines it.)

Mother Victoria:

Mmn! Careful with this Carrickmacross lace! Are His Lordship's shoes cleaned and mended? Buckles shone?

Nellie-Nora: They're nearly ready, Mother Victoria!

Mother Victoria:

Mmn! His Lordship is leaving for Rome on Tuesday!

Brigit: Rome! The lucky beggar!

Mother Victoria:

Did you say something, Brigit?

Brigit: No, Mother! Yes, Mother! I said "Rome", Mother!

Mother Victoria:

His Lordship'll be talking to His Holiness. Maybe he'll say a prayer for you, Brigit! I'll be back!

(Exit Mother Victoria. Women continue to work.)

Brigit: Rome! Sunshine! Wine! And look at us! That rip Victoria! God, how I hate her! Some day I'll put her through the washing machines! Then I'll smather her with red hot irons! Herself and His Lordship with his buckled shoes!

Mandy: Get her keys first, Brigit!

(Brigit moves towards mannikin as she says)

Brigit: Himself with His High Falutin' pretence! Dressing up in foll-de-doll lace and flying off to Rome!

Nellie-Nora: But he's a Prince of the Church, Brigit! Mother Victoria told me!

Brigit: So, Brigit here will be Prince of the Church too! Get me my crozier, Mandy! – The mop! Quick!

(Brigit puts on surplice. Mandy doesn't move.)

Nellie-Nora: Ah, Brigit! be careful!

Brigit: I'll get it myself!

(Nellie-Nora and Mandy watch Brigit. Brigit uses upside down mop as crozier.)

Brigit: Gawd bless you, my scrubbers! Don't squint at me, Nellie-Nora! Stand up straight all of you! Knees together! Say, "Good awfternoon, my Lord!"

Nellie-Nora and Mandy:
Good afternoon, my Lord!

Brigit: Will you forget your bog accents! Say "Good awfternoon, my Lord!"

Nellie-Nora and Mandy:
Good awfternoon, my Lord! *(They bow.)*

Nellie-Nora: What, my Lord, are you doing in Purgatory?

Brigit: A good question! Here's a tenner, Nellie-Nora, for cigarettes. Your favourite Woodbines! I like a smoke myself – a cigar of course! Say "Thank you", Nellie-Nora!

Nellie-Nora: You're very generous, my Lord!

Mandy: What about me, Brigit? – I mean, Bishop, Brigit.

Brigit: My dear, Mandy I bless you! You are now head Bottle-Washer. And you, Nellie-Nora, the Most Reverend Mother! This Big Shiny

	Key (*mop*) opens the pantry and cellar! You'll find plenty of cream-cakes, roast beef, French Wine – and Port!
Mandy:	French Wine! Mmn!
Nellie-Nora:	Roast beef!
Brigit:	Port!

(Mandy finds an underpants. Nellie-Nora lights a cigarette butt.)

| **Mandy**: | My Lord! Your underpants! Freshly starched and trimmed with Carrickmacross lace! |

(Brigit takes underpants and pulls it over Mandy's head.)

| **Brigit**: | I told you, Mandy, that the handling of my underpants is a Mortal Sin! |

(Enter Sister Virginia. Her white veil is pinned back.)

| **Sister Virginia**: | |
| | Brigit! Stop! Stop immediately! |

(Brigit takes off surplice. Nellie-Nora places it on shoulder of mannikin.)

Nellie-Nora:	Yes, Sister Virginia! Sorry, Sister!
Sister Virginia:	
	Please, Mandy! Put that away!
Mandy:	Sorry, Sister Virginia!
Sister Virginia:	
	Mind that cigarette, Nellie-Nora! You might burn the precious Carrickmacross lace!

(The women smile. Keys rattle. Mother Victoria enters with Cathy. Cathy rubs her head and is in tears.)

Mother Victoria:

Back to work immediately, Cathy! You've wasted the morning! Hurry with the Athlone baskets! Hurry! To your tub, Mandy, and tie back that hair! Mmn! – Do I smell cigarettes? Is anyone smoking here, Sister Virginia? Mmn! This area is in a dreadful mess! It's a disgrace! What would His Lordship say?

Have it cleaned immediately, Sister!

Sister Virginia:

Yes, Mother Victoria!

(Exit Mother Victoria. Sister Virginia picks up small threads from floor and exits. Brigit grimaces. Mandy and Nellie-Nora approach Cathy, who stands at table up right of centre.)

Mandy: What happened, Cathy? You didn't – did you – you didn't try it again?

Nellie-Nora: Mother o'God, Cathy! Did you?

Cathy: Mmn! *(Moans)*

(The women resume work. Pause.)

Cathy: *(slowly)* After Mass – while Mother Victoria – was serving Father Durcan's breakfast – I hid in the Confession box! Father Durcan left to collect his car. He never closes the front door. – He drove off without closing the main gate either! I hid behind the beech tree! And I got out! Out on the main road!

Mandy: Outside? Oh, Cathy! Outside!

Cathy: Yes! Outside on the road! But I was like this! No coat! As I walked up the hill, I could smell the sea! The sun was shining on me at last! – A fella passed on a bike – whistling!

Mandy: A fella whistlin'! Oooh, Cathy, what happened? Did you see any smashers when you were out?

Cathy: No smashers, Mandy! No! A few children pointed at me, laughed and called me names. A laundry van passed, turned around and came at me. I fought. I bit them. I screamed. – But they brought me back. – Mother Victoria gave me a mug of strong tea and the usual sermon! *(She rubs her head.)* – But I'm getting out! I'll keep trying! I'm getting out!

Brigit: Bastards! That rip Victoria has her spies everywhere!

(Is interrupted by Sister Virgina who returns with clip-board and pen. Pause. Mother Victoria enters with a bundle of letters.)

Mother Victoria:
Give these letters out at tea-break, Sister! Not until tea-break! His Lordship's linens first! Then the Athlone baskets! They mustn't be delayed!

(Exit Mother Victoria. Brigit looks at Nellie-Nora.)

Brigit: It's a gallon o'bleach I need!

Mandy: To-day is Cathy's birthday, Sister! The letters, please!

Sister Virginia:
Will you not wait? It's almost tea-break, Mandy! *(looks at watch)* These tablecloths must be

Mandy: *(interrupts)* Aah, Sister, please!

Brigit: Do you hear that, Nellie-Nora? His Lordship's tablecloths must be snow-white!

Nellie-Nora: I washed them by hand, Sister!

Brigit: And just the right amount of starch, Nellie-Nora!

Sister Virginia:
Starch, Nellie-Nora?

Nellie-Nora: I starched them myself, Sister!

Sister Virginia:
Thank you, Nellie-Nora!

Brigit: The ironing of His Lordship's tablecloths?

Mandy: The letters, please!

Nellie-Nora: I ironed them too, Sister!

Brigit: Raise up yer hearts, ye washerwomen! The Palace tablecloths are pure-perfect! Alleluia! Alleluia!

(Sister Virginia checks tablecloths as Mandy tries to peep at letters. Tea-bell rings. Sister Virginia gives out letters.)

Sister Virginia:

One for you, Mandy. Posted in New York!

Brigit: From Elvis himself, I suppose!

Sister Virginia:

One for you, Cathy! Look at the size of it!
And one for you, Brigit! Sorry, Nellie-Nora!
None for you.

Nellie-Nora: It's alright, Sister! If I got a letter now, I'd
die of shock! I'll get the tea to-day, Cathy!

(Nellie-Nora exits. Brigit tears open letter, sits on basket down right and reads. Cathy and Mandy turn their backs and open letters. Cathy turns to Sister Virginia.)

Cathy: Look, Sister! From my twins! A beautiful
birthday card! "To Mammy on her birthday.
Love, Michele and Emily."

Sister Virginia:

(sadly) Happy Birthday, Cathy.

(Sister Virginia exits. Cathy stares at card and traces the words with her finger.)

Cathy: Am I ever going to be a mother to them?

(Brigit crumples her letter and stuffs it into her pocket.)

Mandy: He's coming! He's coming to visit! Elvis is
coming!

Brigit: But he was to come last Christmas, Mandy!

Mandy: *(excitedly)* This time Elvis is coming for sure!
My cousin Betty-Ann in America says so!
Look here in this letter! I'll have to get
ready! *(change of tone)* I'll have to be
beautiful for him!

(Nellie-Nora returns with tray on which are old mugs, an old tea-pot and a plate of bread and jam.)

Nellie-Nora: Come on, girls! We'll have a party!

Act 1 Scene 3

(The women take mugs of tea and bread. They eat hungrily. Brigit sits on basket. Mandy sits on ground. Cathy sits on side of table. Nellie-Nora stands. Pause as they eat. Nellie-Nora gives Cathy a small medal.)

Nellie-Nora: It's only a small Holy Medal, Cathy! Wear it around your neck!
Cathy: Thanks, Nellie-Nora! I'll always wear it!
Brigit: A present for you, Cathy! A few love-hearts!
Cathy: Oh, Brigit, thanks!
(Cathy opens paper-bag, takes out a sweet and reads "Forever and ever." Mandy moves towards Cathy.)
Mandy: Happy birthday, Cathy! I made it myself!
It's a pink lacy hanky!
Cathy: It's gorgeous, Mandy! Thanks! Grand-Aunt Elizabeth used to teach me lace-making before I – before I came here!
Mandy: It's only shop-lace, Cathy! Nobody ever taught me how to make lace! – I'd love to make a long lacy dress for myself!
(Mandy moves around rhythmically)
Nellie-Nora: A long lacy dress would suit you, Mandy!
(Cathy is quiet as she looks at presents.)
Mandy: Yes, Nellie-Nora! – Pretend we're in – in Paris! And we're having a huge party for Cathy!
Sound: *(Voice of Elvis "It's now or never!" in distance.)*
Mandy: The moon is shining on the Seine! People sit outside under the stars, drink wine and sing. Painters wear big hats and look for beautiful models.
Brigit: Elvis drops in! Sees our Mandy in her long lacy dress and falls madly in love with her!

Nellie-Nora: They dance all the way to the airport and fly off to Hollywood!

(Mandy, in fantasy, takes up a shirt and dances downstage. Nellie-Nora and Cathy dance and sing. Brigit dances with upside down mop.)

Sound up. *(Voice of Elvis)*
"It's now or never!
Come hold me tight!
Kiss me, my darling.
Be mine to-night.
To-morrow will be too late
It's now or never.
My love won't wait.
When I first saw you
With your smile so tender,
My heart was captured.
My soul surrendered.
I spent a lifetime
Waiting for the right time.
Now that you're near,
The time is here at last.
It's now or never.
Come hold me tight.
Kiss me, my darling.
Be mine to-night.
To-morrow will be too late –
For who knows when
We'll meet again this way."

(Music stops abruptly. Dancing stops. Mandy is disappointed. Pause.)

Cathy: I'd love a slice of home-made cake with sultanas and big juicy cherries!

Mandy Close your eyes and pretend! It'll be true if you pretend!

(The women close their eyes.)

Brigit: Griskeens and black-puddings! The smell of turf-smoke!

Mandy: Frilly fried eggs and potato-cakes!

Nellie-Nora: A big bit o'bacon!

Cathy: Almond icing off the Christmas cake!

Mandy: Flaky and crunchy chocolate!

Nellie-Nora: Loads of big floury potatoes!

Brigit: Smothered in butter!

Mandy: No! With nuts!

Brigit: Potatoes with nuts?

(They laugh.)

Cathy: Read my cup, Nellie-Nora! Here I'll give it another twist!

(Nellie-Nora takes mug. Pause.)

Nellie-Nora: *(hesitantly)* You'll be going on a long journey, Cathy! I see a crowd – a crowd of people! There's a lot of sweetness – lots of letters – and flowers. – Yes – I see sunshine! – Is that alright, Cathy?

Cathy: A long journey? Sweetness, Nellie-Nora? Thanks!

Mandy: Now mine, please! When is he comin'?

(Nellie-Nora is distressed by what she has seen in Cathy's cup/mug.)

Nellie-Nora: Wait a minute, Mandy! – Now – Ohhh, lucky stars are shining for you, Mandy! – Mother o'God, I see diamonds! Lucky diamonds!

Mandy: It must be Elvis! Has he blue-blue eyes? Shiny black hair? He's tall and – slim? Elvis? It is my Elvis!

(Mandy takes cup/mug and looks into it.)

Brigit: Stop, Nellie-Nora! stop!

Mandy:	Ahh, Brigit! Go on, Nellie-Nora! How is he? My Elvis? Isn't he always thinking of me when he sings?
Brigit:	Such fools!
Nellie-Nora:	I'll read your cup, Brigit?
Brigit:	No! Just tell me, that I'll find my baby! Never mind that cup o' tea-leaves!
Mandy:	Do you love your John-Joe, Brigit?
Brigit:	Love? What's love, Mandy? Love's a trick!
Cathy:	Love. Forever and ever!
Mandy:	True Love! *(Sings)*
	"And I give to you
	And you give to me
	Love forever true!"
(speaks)	Richard used to sing that song to me – Every night after the dance he took me home in his shiny red car – We always folded down the seats in the back! – Lovely velvety seats. Every Sunday night! But, when I told him about the baby, he never spoke to me again! Ever! – I only saw him once in the distance after that. Before they brought me here. Oooh! I miss that shiny red car!
Brigit:	Bastard! Didn't I tell you, Mandy! Love is a trick!
Nellie-Nora:	Now you have your own Elvis, Mandy!
Mandy:	Yes I have, Nellie-Nora! He's a smasher! Isn't he? – Why don't you read your own cup, Nellie-Nora?
Nellie-Nora:	Aach! I know what's in my cup, Mandy!

(Work-Bell rings. Nellie-Nora collects tray and exits. She returns quickly and goes to ironing-board down left. Mandy takes out her scrap-book, kisses photographs and immediately

puts it back in apron-pocket. Brigit takes photograph, her paper-baby, from her apron-pocket, stares at it for a moment and returns to work at wash-board up right.

*Machine **sound** up. Time passing. **Lights** lower.)*

*Straight into **Act 1 Scene 4 True Love**.*

Act 1 Scene 4

TRUE LOVE

Set same as for Act 1 Scene 3. Purple drapes folded on shelves. Brigit, Cathy, Mandy and Nellie-Nora on stage. Sister Virginia enters with Juliet, a seventeen-year old girl. Juliet carries a bundle of linen. Sister Virginia takes a white apron from a hook and gives it to Juliet .

Sister Virginia:

This is Juliet. She'll be working with you for the next few months.

(Women stare at Juliet.)

Brigit: They're getting younger all the time! When is it arriving, Juliet?

Juliet: When is what arriving?

Nellie-Nora: The baby of course!

(Nellie-Nora takes bundle of linen from Juliet.)

Sister Virginia:

Juliet is from the orphanage! No baby, Nellie-Nora!

Cathy: Hello, Juliet!

Mandy: Juliet!

Nellie-Nora: Welcome, Juliet!

Brigit: Howya!

Cathy: The orphanage? St. Anthony's?

Juliet: Yes!

Cathy: Do you know my Michele and Emily? My twins? They're six years old. Do you know them?

Juliet: Oh! The twins! Blonde curly hair and blue eyes?

Cathy: Tell me about them please!

Juliet: Have you not seen them lately?

Cathy: No! No, Juliet! Are they growing fast? Do they eat enough?

Juliet: Yes! They're growing very fast. They'll be making their First Holy Communion next year!

Cathy: My babies making First Holy Communion! I must see my babies!

Sister Virginia:

(gently) Will you check the Athlone blankets for me, Cathy? Please? – Now we'll fold the sheets, Juliet. First we find the code. It's in the corner in red thread – see! We fold carefully this way. Corners together so!

(They stand down centre and fold sheets rhythmically. Women work in background.)

Sister Virginia:

You're seventeen now, Juliet. Have you been out at all – outside?

Juliet: No, Sister! I don't want to live out there!

Sister Virginia:

Why, Juliet? Your life's ahead of you!

Juliet: My Mammy lived here until she died. I want to stay in here!

Sister Virginia:

But you can't make a choice until you've been out.

Juliet: I'd hate to live out there! All those men!

Sister Virginia:

What men, Juliet? There are fathers and mothers, brothers and sisters – families!

Juliet: But look what happened to Mammy! No! No babies for me!

Sister Virginia:
Most men are good, Juliet!

Juliet: They're not! Men are oversexed! Mother Joachim said so, when I was working in the convent!

Sister Virginia:
Mother Joachim! Why did she say that?

Juliet: When I answered the side-door. When I screamed!

Sister Virginia:
You screamed! But why? Tell me, Juliet!

Juliet: You see, Mick, the vegetable man! He grabbed me here! Pushed me against the wall. Said he'd murder me – break my neck if I moved! Old Mother Benedict was just in time! She hit him a wollop with her big rosary beads, but Mother Joachim wouldn't believe me – that I didn't lead him on!

Sister Virginia:
(lifting sheets) He was just one man, Juliet! You mustn't stay in here! Take a job outside! Go away and see new places! Read the great books! Earn your own money. We're on an island here!

Juliet: But, Sister, I was never on a bus or a train! I'd be afraid!

Sister Virginia:
Put the sheets on the shelves now, Juliet. Cathy will give you something to sew. I'll – We'll pray for you.

Juliet: Thank you, Sister!

(Sister Virginia moves towards Cathy.)

Sister Virginia:

        Will you give Juliet something to sew,
Cathy? *(Lowers her voice.)* See that she eats,
that she finishes her meals.

Cathy: Yes, Sister! Can you sew on buttons, Juliet?

Juliet: Yes, Cathy!

Nellie-Nora: Look, Sister! More shirts from the seminary!

(Nellie-Nora gives Sister a bundle of white shirts. Sister Virginia examines them.)

Sister Virginia:

        Mmn! Buttons missing!

Juliet: Would there be many students in the
seminary, Sister?

Sister Virginia:

        Yes, Juliet! Nearly every mother west of the
Shannon has a son studying for the
priesthood. Where I grew up all the fine
young men enter a seminary!

Juliet: They never go out in the world?

Sister Virginia:

        Some go to Maynooth. Others prepare for
the Foreign Missions.

Juliet: I'd like that! Teaching black babies!

Mandy: All those nice young men! What a waste!

Sister Virginia:

        They go to the Far East. Others to the
States. Some to Africa. My three uncles, my
cousin in Galway and my brother John are
priests. Grand Aunt Teresa and Aunt Mary
are nuns. The Island of Saints and Scholars
is now an island of priests and nuns.

Cathy: My Uncle Jeremiah is a Canon!

Brigit: For all the good that'll do you, Cathy! Sure

	my uncle is an Archbishop and look at me!
Sister Virginia:	
	Will you help sew buttons on the shirts, Brigit?
Brigit:	Buttons! Yes, Sister! I'll sew on a hundred buttons, if you give me the keys!
Sister Virginia:	
	You know I can't –
Brigit:	Ah, Sister! This letter I got from my cousin Katie in Cillnamona says that John-Joe is getting married next week! He doesn't know about Rosa! She's his baby too, Sister! I have to tell him! Please, Sister! The keys!
Sister Virginia:	
	I can't, Brigit! I'm not in charge! – I'm sorry!

(Sister Virginia exits.)

Brigit: Bloody nuns! They dont give a damn! Damn! Damn! Damn His Lordship! Damn the Pope and all the bloody lot o' them!

(Juliet moves closer to Cathy.)

Juliet: Did you know my Mammy, Julia Mannion?

Cathy: Julia Mannion! Yes! I was with her when – she – got the heart attack.

Juliet: They wouldn't let me see her!

Cathy: We'll look after you, Juliet!

(Brigit examines a seminary shirt.)

Brigit: A hedge-tear in a seminary shirt!

Mandy: They play football and hurling, Brigit!

Brigit: Hurlin's smashin'! I played camogie at school! Got my head opened once! I had to get thirteen stitches!

Mandy: Football's better! All those lads rollin' around in the mud cursin' and swearin'!

Nellie-Nora: Better than kickin' people!

(*Cathy has a bad attack of coughing, but says*)

Cathy: My head! Oh, my head! Oh, God!

(*Cathy holds head in her hands and sways in pain.*)

Brigit: Take a rest, Cathy!

Nellie-Nora: Stop the sewing, Cathy!

Mandy: Is it the asthma, Cathy?

Cathy: I'll ask Sister Virginia for an aspirin!

(*Cathy stumbles to door and exits.*)

Mandy: She needs more than aspirin!

Juliet: What's wrong with Cathy? She's not dyin', is she?

Nellie-Nora: Cathy's worn out, Juliet! Her heart's broke!

Brigit: Wasn't it a rotten bastard, who left her in the lurch! Cathy never talks about him!

Nellie-Nora: She keeps quiet about him!

Juliet: Who is he?

Brigit: The father of her twins! Told nobody! – Some Big Shot, I suppose!

Nellie-Nora: Sure, maybe he's married!

Brigit: Or a Bishop!

Mandy: Or a film-star!

Brigit: Seven years without tellin' anyone! Women are fools!

Mandy: Would you like to see my scrap-book, Juliet?

(*Mandy takes scrap-book from apron pocket.*)

Juliet: What's in it? – Oh, snaps! I've snaps too! In my prayer-book!

Mandy: Of Elvis?

Juliet: No! Of Audrey Hepburn!

Mandy: Audrey Hepburn?

Juliet: Yes! She's so thin! You see, she doesn't eat bread or potatoes! That's why! Oooh, I'd love to be that thin!

Brigit: But you're as thin as a wisp, Juliet!

Juliet: No! I'm not! I'm huge!

(Enter Sister Virginia and Cathy. Mandy hides scrap-book.)
Sister Virginia:

Take it easy with the mending, Cathy.
Nellie-Nora: Yes, Cathy! I'll help you in a minute!
Cathy: Thanks!
(Mother Victoria enters, walks downstage, beads and keys rattling. She beckons to Sister Virginia.)
Mother Victoria:

There's a visitor, a Father McCarthy, to see you, Sister Virginia! Says he's a friend of your brother, Father John! I've told them in the kitchen. Tea in the small parlour. Ten minutes. I'll give you ten minutes. And remember. Custody of the eyes, Sister! I'll see you afterwards in the cloister.

Sister Virginia:

Thank you, Mother Victoria!
(Sister brings forward her veil, unhooks her outerskirt, puts on big sleeves and exits.)
Mother Victoria:

We'll say the Rosary together for a special intention. "Thou, O Lord wilt open my lips."
Brigit: But we said the Rosary while we were ironing the sheets for His Lordship's Palace! Five and a half decades, Mother!
Mandy: And Nellie-Nora offered them up for His Lordship, Mother!
Mother Victoria:

Very good indeed, Nellie-Nora! I'll say my office here. You may sing hymns if you wish. Softly please! Hmmmm *(She intones)* "The bells of the Angelus are calling to pray. In sweet tones announcing the sacred Ave Ave, Ave, Ave Maria. Ave, Ave, Ave Maria."

(Brigit sings in contrast but uses same tune.)

"On top of old Smokey
All covered with snow.
I lost my true lover
From courtin' too slow."

Mother Victoria:

Aperi, Domine, os nostrum ad benedicendum
nomen sanctum tuum – Stop that rubbish!
Stop, Brigit! You're a disgrace! In front of
this innocent young girl too! – How do you
like the laundry, Juliet?

Juliet: 'Tis – alright, Mother Victoria! Thank you!

Mother Victoria:

Very good, Juliet! Is His Lordship's linen
ready, Brigit? Tablecloths for the crimson
gold dining-room? Did you double-check
the mending?

Brigit: Aren't we busy with the Athlone scrubbin',
Mother Victoria?

Mother Victoria:

His Lordship must be looked after first!
Remember he's a Prince of the Church!

(Brigit and Nellie-Nora exchange smiles.)
Mother Victoria walks to and fro downstage. Slight pause.)

Mother Victoria:

Aperi, Domine, os nostrum ad benedicendum
nomen sanctum tuum: numda quoque or
nostrum ab omnibus vanis, perversis et
alienis cogitationibus: intellectus illumina/

Brigit: Nellie-Nora is knitting crimson combinations
for His Lordship to keep him comfortable
during those chilly evenings in Rome. Isn't
that right, Nellie-Nora?

(Nellie-Nora is in shock. Mother Victoria looks at Nellie-Nora. Pause.)

Nellie-Nora: It's not a combinations, Mother! It's a jumper!

(Mother Victoria continues to walk to and fro as she reads office.)

Mother Victoria:

        – Ab omnibus vais, perversis et alienis cogitationibus: intellectus illumina, affectus inflamma, ut digne, attende ac devote hoc beatae Virginis Mariae valeamus et exaudiri mereamur ante divinae conspectum Majestatis tuae –

Brigit:

        "On top of Old Smokey
        All covered with snow,
        I lost my true lover
        From courtin' too slow."

Mother Victoria:

        Per Christum Dominum nostrum!
        I'm saying my office, Brigit! Mmmn!
        Mmmn!

Brigit: Yes, Mother! I'm sorry, Mother!

(Mother Victoria exits in disgust. Pause. Brigit takes a piece of linen, puts it on her head and imitating Mother Victoria's walk and voice says,)

Brigit: I'm saying my office, Brigit!

(Women continue to wash, iron and sew.)

Cathy: *(sings softly)*
        "And I give to you
        And you give to me
        Love forever true." –

Brigit: Love forever true? Huhh!

(Lights down. Brigit, Cathy, Nellie-Nora and Mandy freeze. Machine sounds up for three seconds, then fade as Plain Chant Credo comes up. Mother Victoria stands for a moment at doorway upstage, inspects women, then exits.)

Act 1 Scene 5

CREDO SCENE

Sound: One soprano voice sings
"Credo in unum Deum,
Patrem omnipotentem,
Factorem coeli et terrae,
Visibilium omnium et invisibilium.
Et in unum Dominum, Jesum Christum,
Filium Dei unigenitum.
Et ex Patre natum ante omnia saecula.
Deum de Deo, lumen de lumine.
Deum verum de Deo vero, genitum non factum,
Consubstantialem Patri –

(Stage in darkness except highlight on Sister Virginia as she enters "convent chapel". She dips finger in Holy Water Font and makes Sign of Cross. Glow from stained-glass windows and Sanctuary Lamp. Sister Virginia walks downstage and kneels. She then lies prostrate, arms spread out in shape of cross for five seconds. She kneels in highlight and prays the Credo.)

Sister Virginia:
I believe in God the Father Almighty,
Creator of Heaven and earth and in Jesus
Christ His only Son Our Lord, who was
conceived by the Holy Ghost – I believe
in God – God? – I believe in God – I try –
I believe in God the Father Almighty,

Creator of Heaven and earth and in Jesus
Christ His only Son Our Lord, who was
conceived by the Holy Ghost, born of the
Virgin Mary –

Voice of Brigit:

Keys, Sister! My John-Joe is getting married
next week! He doesn't know about our baby!

Sister Virginia:

Creator of Heaven and earth and in Jesus
Christ His only Son Our Lord who was
conceived –

Voice of Brigit:

Keys! My baby, Rosa! I have to find my
baby!

Sister Virginia:

Born of the Virgin Mary, suffered under
Pontius Pilate was crucified, died and was
buried –

(*Sound of Cathy's breathing during asthma attack.*)

Voice of Mandy:

It's Cathy! She's chokin', Sister!

Voice of Nellie-Nora:

A kettle! Steam! Hurry, Sister! Hurry!

Sister Virginia:

Was crucified, died and was buried. He
descended into Hell.

Voice of Mother Victoria:

Mandy thought she could leave if she wasn't
pregnant, so she performed an abortion on
herself!

Sister Virginia:

He descended into Hell. The third day He
arose from the dead.

Voice of Mother Victoria:

We give them food, shelter and clothing.

We look after their spiritual needs. No one
else wants them! No one else wants them!

Sister Virginia:

The third day He arose from the dead. –

Voice of Mother Victoria:

A vow of Obedience, Sister! Blind
Obedience!

Sister Virginia:

The third day he arose –

Sister Virginia:

Is it just a story from the East – from St.
Paul?
A story? – The women need help from you,
the Risen! But, did you rise from the dead? –
You're supposed to be a Loving Father! Are
you a God of Love? – A God of Justice? –
I thought I'd be working for the poor! Am I
being brain-washed? Will I become
dehumanised too, if I stay here long enough?
Locked in by Obedience? The Rule? Why
are there changes in Our Holy Founder's
Book? Was early Christian History rewritten
too? Woman's witness submerged? – Christ
Crucified! Help them! For a woman bore
you, carried you for nine months! Mother
of Jesus, do something about Cathy, Mandy,
Nellie-Nora and the others! When you arose
from that tomb, women were your first
witnesses! Your first miracle was performed
at your Mother's request! – Help us! –
Help me!

*(Sister Virginia makes sign of Cross, stands and exits. Lights
up for **Act 1 Scene 6 Effigy**)*

Act 1 Scene 6

EFFIGY

Hum of huge washing-machines. Bleach smells. Brigit and Mandy work at wash-tubs with wash-boards right of centre. Nellie-Nora at ironing-board down left. Mannikin dressed in Bishop's soutane (surplice folded across shoulder) up left. Cathy and Juliet are mending at work-table up centre. Large Laundry Basket down right. Linens on shelves up centre. Mannikin's head on lower shelf. Cathy has breathing difficulties.

Brigit: Spit out your troubles, Cathy! They'll rot your brain if you don't! 'Tis far from this dirt you were reared!

Cathy: Thanks, Brigit!

Nellie-Nora: Troubles you can't talk about – they're the bad ones *(shows Cathy a small mirror.)* I'm tellin' you, Cathy, you're better lookin' than Grace Kelly! Sure if Cary Grant, Bing Crosby or Frank Sinatra himself saw you, they'd all fall in love with you!

Mandy: But not Elvis! Remember he's mine! He belongs to me!

Cathy: You can keep your Elvis, Mandy! Thanks, Nellie-Nora!

Mandy: Elvis! That voice! Just to see him would be heaven!

Nellie-Nora: We'll all go to heaven when we die!

Brigit: Mmnn! What the hell good will that be?

Mandy: I want my heaven now with Elvis!

(Mandy takes out her scrap-book and examines snapshots.)

Mandy: I'll ask Sister Virginia for snaps of Elvis! And one of Frank Sinatra for you, Cathy!

Cathy: Sister Virginia is not allowed look at filmstars.

Brigit: Only at Father Durcan! Some filmstar that fella! Face like the back of a bus!

Nellie-Nora: Mother o'God, Brigit! Don't forget he gave us the old radio!

Mandy: I could write to Elvis in Hollywood!

Brigit: No! Not again!

(Nellie-Nora blesses herself.)

Mandy: Juliet! Will you give me a pencil! Quick!

Juliet: You're going to write to a filmstar in America? Will he get the letter?

Mandy: Of course he will! Elvis gets all my letters!

(Juliet gives pencil to Mandy and looks on as Mandy writes.)

Mandy: Now! *(Slowly as she writes)*
"My dearest Elvis, Thank you for your beeeautiful wonderful photo! I'll keep it under my pillow! Please send me more photos of yourself for my scrap-book too. You're gorgeous! All my love and – a hundred kisses!

Juliet: A hundred kisses?

(Mandy puts crosses on letter.)

Mandy: Yours forever! – No! Yours forever and ever and ever! Your darling Mandy! Kiss! Kiss! Kiss!

Nellie-Nora: Your sweetheart sounds nicer!

Juliet: Maggie Brennan was writing a letter to a boy and she wrote S.W.A.L.K. – sealed with a loving kiss! Will you put that in too, Mandy?

Mandy: Yes! That's a great idea!

(Mandy writes S.W.A.L.K. She and Juliet giggle. Brigit is scornful.)

Brigit: Yours until hell freezes! And now the address! Your address, Mandy? Your address?

(Brigit snaps letter and reads)

Brigit: Saint Paul's Home for Penitent Women! Home for the unwanted. The outcasts! Saint Paul's Home for the women nobody wants!

Mandy: No, Brigit! No! Give me my letter!

(Brigit and Mandy push one another. Mandy falls to floor.)

Brigit: How do you think that sounds? What'll he think? Ha? You'd be finished with him! Finished forever and ever!

Mandy: *(sobbing)* No, Brigit! No address! Elvis will find me! Elvis will find his Mandy!

Brigit: Nobody wants you! Nobody wants any of us!

(Brigit throws letter on floor. Cathy stares at Brigit. Nellie-Nora walks towards Brigit.)

Nellie-Nora: Brigit!

(Brigit catches Cathy's accusing eye.)

Nellie-Nora: *(Louder)* Brigit!

(Pause.)

Brigit: I'm sorry, Mandy!

(Pause.)

Brigit: Sorry! I'm really sorry!

(Juliet picks up letter and tries to comfort Mandy. Nellie-Nora lights a cigarette and offers it to Mandy, who is very distressed.)

Juliet: I'll write the address for you, Mandy.

(Juliet writes)

Juliet: Ireland!

(Pause. Brigit moves towards basket.)

Brigit: I've a great idea! We'll post Mandy off to Hollywood! Come on, Mandy!

Mandy: No! No! Leave me alone, Brigit!

47

Brigit: Into this basket with you, Mandy! Give us a hand, Nellie-Nora!

(Brigit opens basket and moves it down centre stage.)

Nellie-Nora: Yes, Mandy! Come on!

Brigit: Hop in, Mandy! Now's your chance! Off to Hollywood! Come on, Cathy! We'll pack her off to the U.S.A.!

(Mandy reluctantly gets into basket.)

Brigit: Let down your hair!

(Mandy unties her long hair.)

Mandy: How do I look?

Nellie-Nora: You look gorgeous! Just like a filmstar!

Brigit: Off you go! First class!

Nellie-Nora: Watch that door, Juliet!

Brigit: Are you ready, Mandy?

(Brigit and Nellie-Nora hum as they move the basket to and fro to the tune of "Wooden Heart".)

Nellie-Nora: Are you watching that door, Juliet?

(Juliet is more interested in business with basket.)

Juliet: I am, Nellie-Nora!

(Mandy twirls in basket.)

Mandy: But, Brigit! Where's my Elvis?

Brigit: Wait a minute, Mandy! Where's our Wooden Heart Fella?

(Brigit rushes upstage to mannikin. She takes off soutane and surplice, throws them on table, stands behind mannikin and walks it towards Mandy in basket.)

Brigit: *(Elvis Voice)* Hi there, Mandy! You sure are lookin' pretty to-day! *(own voice)* Help me, Cathy, Nellie-Nora! Help me to dress him up like a "Big Shot Filmstar"!

(They giggle and laugh.)

Nellie-Nora: Hurry! Give us a shirt, Cathy!

Mandy: Yes! A colourdy shirt, Cathy! A gorgeous shirt for my Elvis!

(Cathy moves to shelves and finds a multi-coloured shirt.)
Cathy: Here's a nice cotton shirt, Mandy!
Mandy: A tie! He needs a tie!
(Brigit searches shelves and finds a blue tie.)
Mandy: A Paris Blue tie for my Elvis!
Mandy: Trousers!
(Nellie-Nora finds trousers on a lower shelf.)
Mandy: Oh no! Not those old trousers!
Nellie-Nora: These are great trousers, Mandy! Hold him up and we'll put them on!
(They pull on trousers and lift mannikin into basket as Mandy complains.)
Mandy: His head! He has no head! Elvis's head?
Cathy: Get that old head from the press, Nellie-Nora!
(As Brigit and Cathy button shirt and zip trousers, Nellie-Nora finds old head and puts it on mannikin.)
Juliet: He's like a doll! He is!
Nellie-Nora: Stay at that door, Juliet!
Mandy: His hair! His black shiny hair!
Brigit: Hair? What will we do about hair?
Juliet: Shhh! There's someone comin' down the corridor!
Brigit: Take her out! Quick!
Cathy: Out of the basket! Hurry, Mandy!
(The women, in a state of panic, close the basket on the Elvis figure. His head protrudes. They return to work. Pause. Brigit exits towards cloister. Pause. She returns.)
Brigit: False alarm! Come on, girls! Hair for this beautiful bachelor from Hollywood! Hurry. Take him out of the basket.
Cathy: What about a piece of Mother Victoria's winter shawl?
Nellie-Nora: No! Mother o'God! No! Just pretend, Mandy! Pretend he has beautiful black shiny hair! Now, Mandy, back into the basket!

(Mandy steps into basket. She covers her eyes with her hands.)

Mandy: Yes, Nellie-Nora! Yes! Now I can see his shiny hair! And look, Cathy! His eyes! His gorgeous come-to-bed eyes!

Cathy: He has long curly eye-lashes, Mandy!

(They laugh.)

Mandy: And lips! Big and wide!

Cathy: Smiling! a dimple in his chin!

Nellie-Nora: And clean fingernails!

Cathy: A gold pin for his Paris Blue Tie!

(Cathy takes a hairgrip from her hair and fastens his tie.)

Brigit: Ears! For whisperin' in!

Juliet: He's very nice, Mandy!

Nellie-Nora: Stay at that door, Juliet!

Mandy: Yes! Isn't he a smasher, girls?

Cathy: He needs a pure silk hanky!

Brigit: Where's that purply hanky, Cathy: Wait a minute – here it is!

(Cathy fixes silk hanky in shirt-pocket.)

Juliet: A pure silk hanky?

Brigit: Now, Mandy! Here's your Elvis!

(Mandy stares at mannikin, kisses it.)

Mandy: *(sings)*
"Have I told you lately
That I love you?
Could I tell you once again somehow?
Have I told with all my heart and soul
That I adore you?
Well, Darlin', I'm tellin' you now!".

(Mandy hugs mannikin as she sings. Women watch her, then they return to work. Lights are rose-coloured.)

Brigit: He's askin' you to marry him, Mandy!

Mandy: I will! Oh, yes! I will!

Nellie-Nora: I've a great idea! We'll dress Mandy for her

weddin'! Hurry! Hurry! Mother o'God!
He might change his mind!

(Cathy takes Mandy's white apron and fastens it veil-like on her hair, then drapes a long white sheet over her shoulders as a train. Juliet helps.)

Cathy: A pure white veil! A long satin train!

Juliet: You're very posh, Mandy!

Nellie-Nora: You look gorgeous, Mandy!

Mandy: I am! I'm gorgeous!

Brigit: Remember! I'm the Bishop! I'll do this important wedding!

(Brigit moves table to left-centre, jumps on to table and dresses in crimson soutane. She puts surplice/mitre on her head, while women finish dressing Elvis. They lift Elvis into basket beside Mandy and sing)

"Daisy, Daisy!
Give me your answer. Do!
I'm half crazy all for the love of you!
It won't be a stylish marriage.
We can't afford a carriage
Won't you look neat upon the seat of a
bicycle made for two?"

(Brigit deepens her voice as she says)

Brigit: Silence!

(The women push basket towards Bishop/Brigit. Juliet holds long train.)

Brigit: Do you, Mandy Prenderville, take this Elvis Presley as your lawful husband to have and to hold in sickness and in health until death do you part?

Mandy: I do! Oh, yes! I do!

Brigit: And now, Elvis Presley, do you –

Mandy: *(interrupts)* But, Brigit, his real name is Elvis Aron Garon Presley!

Brigit: Do you, Elvis Aron Garon Presley, take

Mandy Prenderville -

Nellie-Nora: He does! He does!

Brigit: Don't interrupt, Nellie-Nora!

(The women smile.)

Brigit: Do you, Elvis Aron Garon Presley, take Mandy Prenderville as your lawful wedded wife to have and to hold in sickness and in health until death do you part?

(Nellie-Nora rocks Elvis's head in assent. Cathy is in tears. Sister Virginia stands at doorway in background, but the women do not notice her.)

Brigit: I now pronounce you man and wife. Bless you!

Nellie-Nora, Brigit and Cathy: Congratulations, Mandy!

(Mandy begins to kiss Elvis, but Brigit interrupts)

Brigit: You – may kiss the bride, Elvis Aron Garon Presley!

(Mandy kisses Elvis. The women cheer.)

Nellie-Nora: Have as many babies as you want now, Mandy!

(Sister Virginia exits.)

Nellie-Nora: A honeymoon! We'll send them on their honeymoon!

Mandy: *(sings)*
"My heart would break in two
If I should lose you
I'm no good
Without you anyhow!
Dear, have I told you lately
That I love you?
Well, Darlin' I'm tellin' you now!"

(Mandy hugs Elvis as she sings. The women push basket in a circular movement and sing with Mandy)

"Have I told you lately that I love you?
Could I tell you once again somehow?
Have I told with all my heart and soul
How I adore you?
Well, Darlin', I'm tellin' you now!
Tellin' you now!
Have I told you lately when I'm sleepin'?
Every dream I dream is you somehow?
Have I told you why the nights are long
when you're not with me?
Well, Darlin', I'm tellin' you now.
Tellin' you now!"

(Lights down as Elvis's voice comes up over women singing.)
Elvis sings

"Dear, have I told you lately
That I love you
Could I tell you once again somehow
Have I told with all my heart and soul
That I adore you
Well, Darlin', I'm tellin' you now!
Tellin' you now.
My heart would break
In two if I should lose you.
I'm no good without you anyhow!" etc.

(Continue during interval.)

INTERVAL

Act 2 Scene 1

OFFICE 1

Sound: Plain Chant "Magnificat". One soprano voice.
"Magnificat anima mea Dominum.
Et exultavit Spiritus meus. In Deo salutari
meo.
Quia respexit humilitatem ancillae suae.
Ecce enim ex hoc beatam me dicent omnes
generationes.
Quia fecit mihi magna qui potens est
et sanctum nomen ejus. – "

Small office in convent laundry. Mother Victoria sits on high-backed chair at desk up centre. Two bibles, a telephone, keys, a crucifix and office book on desk. A stool at right of desk. Photographs of Bishops and a Pope on walls. If using same set as in laundry workspace, a chair, small table with telephone and stool will do. Lighting effects change the set. A gentle knock is heard.

Mother Victoria:
Come in!
(Sister Virginia enters quietly. Her veil covers her shoulders. big sleeves cover her arms and hands. She carries a box of Black Magic chocolates in her big sleeves. She kneels on floor. The phone rings. Mother Victoria answers. Plain Chant fades.)

Mother Victoria:
Yes! – Yes, Father! I'll hold on! – Oh! –
Good morning, my Lord! – Yes! – I'm

> working on the ledgers now! – I should
> have them finished by to-morrow, my Lord!
> – I'll send on the cheque too! – Thank you,
> my Lord!

(She smiles as she puts down phone.)

Mother Victoria:

> You may sit down, Sister!

(Sister Virginia remains on her knees and takes a box of Black Magic chocolates from her big sleeves.)

Sister Virginia:

> Thank you, Mother Victoria! May I keep
> and dispose of this box of chocolates?

Mother Victoria:

> Chocolates? Black Magic Chocolates?
> Mmmn? Did that seminarian give you
> chocolates, Sister?

Sister Virginia:

> Yes, Mother Victoria!

Mother Victoria:

> Aaam! Yes! You may dispose of them! Sit
> down, Sister!

(Sister Virginia sits on stool.)

Mother Victoria:

> How do you like the laundry? A change
> from Spiritual Year in the Novitiate, I'm
> sure! Are you happy? Tell me!

Sister Virginia:

> The work – the women – I find it difficult,
> Mother!

Mother Victoria:

> Difficult, Sister!

Sister Virginia:

> Yes, Mother! – It's very sad!

Mother Victoria:

> Sad, Sister? You find them sad?

Sister Virginia:

Yes, Mother! The women need their children! – Is it really necessary to keep them locked away?

Mother Victoria:

Those women can't be trusted! They're weak, Sister! No control! They've broken the sixth and ninth Commandments!

Sister Virginia:

But isn't our God a Loving Father, a Forgiving Father? The men, who made them pregnant, broke the same Commandments!

(Mother Victoria stands and walks around office.)

Mother Victoria:

Men? You don't understand, Sister! No one wants those women! We protect them from their passions! We give them food, shelter and clothing! We look after their spiritual needs!

Sister Virginia:

They need medicines – vitamins, fresh air, sunshine! – Cathy's asthma! The attacks are more frequent! Brigit mourns the baby she gave up for adoption! She's a bitter woman! The others are –

Mother Victoria:

Well, Sister?

Sister Virginia:

Cathy has a constant headache, Mother Victoria.

Mother Victoria:

Headache, Sister?

Sister Virginia:

Cathy told me – you hit her around the

head, when the van-men brought her back yesterday.

Mother Victoria:

Cathy was hysterical! I had to slap her – to – bring her back to reality!

Sister Virginia:

I'm very worried about her. She needs help. She's very low in spirits!

Mother Victoria:

Custody of the eyes. You forget yourself, Sister! You are preparing to take vows! A Vow of Obedience! I know Cathy's tricks! She's a bit of an actress! She exaggerates! Give her a tonic! A spoonful three times a day. It'll build her up.

(Mother Victoria stands in shadows behind chair.)

Mother Victoria:

When I was nineteen, I had the same thoughts! I wanted to free the penitents – mothers of some of the women in the laundry now. You see, this weakness to sins of the flesh stays in the blood for seven generations! When you take Vows, Sister, you'll receive Grace and Understanding. Keep aloof from those fallen women! St. Paul says "People who do wrong will not inherit the Kingdom of Heaven. – People of immoral lives – fornicators, adulterers."

Sister Virginia:

But St. Paul hated women! – Christ had many women friends!

Mother Victoria:

St. Paul, Sister! St. Paul may have been afraid of women! Women tempt men! Remember the Garden! Eve started it all!

Sister Virginia:

Eve? The Garden, Mother?

Mother Victoria:

Don't interrupt, Sister! Those women can
be treacherous! I warn you to be careful in
the laundry!

Sister Virginia:

They won't harm me, Mother Victoria!

Mother Victoria:

Just be careful, when Brigit is using bleach!
Sister Luke has permanent scars on her face
and hands!

Sister Virginia:

If I were Brigit or Cathy and my babies
were taken from me, I'd tear down the walls
with my nails! *(interrupted by)*

Mother Victoria:

Calm yourself, Sister! Calm! Wisdom will
be given to you! Grace to do God's will.
God's ways are not our ways! I'll pray for
you!

(Mother Victoria sits at desk and faces Sister Virginia.)

Mother Victoria:

Have you been meditating properly, Sister?

Sister Virginia:

I try, Mother! But there are dark – dark
clouds – doubts, Mother! The women are
drudges, are bond-women! I – I didn't
expect this!

Mother Victoria:

Doubts, Sister! We all go through those dark
nights! – Dark Nights! Try to remember
that We Are Eclipsed! But that deep inside
there is a Shining that is Immortal – a part
of us, which is outside Time. Hold on to

that thought! Do not question the System!
You want to change the Rule, the Church,
the World! You must start with yourself!
Change yourself first! Get rid of Pride! Obey
the Rule, Sister! Remember
– We are eclipsed. But Blind
Obedience will carry you through!

Sister Virginia:

But, Mother Victoria! – Thank you,
Mother! – I'll – I'll try!

(Sister Virginia leaves office as lights change.
Plain Chant "Magnificat" sung by one soprano voice.)

Magnificat continued
"Fecit potentiam in bracchio suo:
dispersit superbos mente cordis sui.
Deposuit potentes de sede et exaltavit
humiles.
Esurientes implevit bonis: et divites dimisit
inanes.
Suscepit Israel puerum suum, recordatus
misericordiae suae. – "

*(Fade to machine-**sounds**.)*

61

Act 2 Scene 2

FLOOR

Sound: *Machine-sound up.*

Enter Cathy, Nellie-Nora, Brigit, Mandy and Sister Virginia to set of Office 1. Table up left. Nellie-Nora places large dustbin centre stage. Mandy and Brigit exit with chair and stool. They return immediately with sweeping-brushes, polishing-cloths. Sister Virginia pins back her veil and hooks up her skirt. Cathy brings on old wooden polishing-blocks and tin of polish. Mandy washes floor upstage with mop and bucket of water. Sister Virginia stands and watches.

Brigit: It'd take more than soap and water to clean up this place!

(The women sweep floor rhythmically. Cathy has attack of coughing. Cathy takes a polishing-block.)

Cathy: We need a machine for polishing instead of these old wooden blocks, Sister!

Brigit: We're the machines, Cathy!

Sister Virginia:

I'll speak to Mother Victoria about new equipment, Cathy!

(Cathy tries to use heavy polishing-block, but continues to cough. Sister Virginia takes block from Cathy and polishes down left beside Brigit. Nellie-Nora sweeps up right.)

Sister Virginia:

Take a rest, Cathy!

(Cathy sits on table up left. Church bell rings.)

Brigit: The prayer-bell, Sister! Shouldn't you be on your knees in the chapel instead of in here?

Sister Virginia:

To work is to pray, Brigit!

Brigit: We'll go straight up so. Won't we?

(After prayer-bell is heard, the rhythm of sweeping and polishing changes to rhythm of tune, which Cathy is humming, "The Irish Washerwoman" She uses table-top or washboard as bodhran percussion. Lighting changes to warmer tones.)

Brigit: Work! Work! Work! Work is God here! Washing, scrubbing, washing, scrubbing, scrubbing, labouring! *(rhythmically as she polishes)*

Nellie-Nora: Cigarette! Where did I put the matches? *(No answer.)*

Juliet: Where will I put the dust? *(No answer.)*

(Nellie-Nora lights cigarette butt. Puffs of smoke. Mandy kneels down centre, presses a polishing-cloth to her nose.)

Mandy: Oomn! I love perfumy wax. Look! It's getting nice and shiny! Like a dance-hall floor! Look!

(Mandy begins to waltz-dance as Cathy hums. Others polish and brush to rhythm of Cathy's humming, which now grows slightly faster.)

Mandy: Ahh, but no fellas!

Brigit: No fellas! No trouble you mean! Do you hear me, Mandy?

Mandy: Still – nice trouble, Brigit!

(Brigit takes Mandy's polishing-cloth, stands behind dust-bin facing audience. Crimson high-light on dust-bin.)

Brigit: Into the bin goes Mandy! *(throws cloth into bin. Others continue to polish-sweep.)*

Brigit: Bin gobbles her up!

(She takes Cathy's cloth and throws it in.)

Brigit: Bin gobbles up Cathy! Look at the smoke and flames rising from his huge jaws! Bin waits for your white bones, Sister Virginia!

Sister Virginia:

> I'm not ready for Purgatory yet, Saint Peter! There are things I must do here first!

Nellie-Nora: *(chants)* Purgatory is a place or state of punishment, where some souls suffer for a time before they can enter Heaven!

Brigit: *(looks into bin)* Richard's in here, Mandy! Come on! Have a look!

Mandy: No! No, Brigit! I don't want to see him!

(Mandy continues to waltz-dance around stage. Rhythm grows faster.)

Brigit: Hello, Mandy! Hello, Richard! It's gettin' hotter, is it? Did His Lordship arrive yet, Richard? He did! He's in there! Good! In you go, Nellie-Nora!

(Brigit takes dust from Juliet and throws it into bin.)

Brigit: Mandy and Richard are waltzin' away in the red-hot flames!

(Rhythm of music grows faster. Brigit takes a brush and bangs it into bin.)

Brigit: Ha, Mother Victoria! No! Not in here! You've to go to the other place! The hotter place! No, Mother Victoria, I've no keys! No keys for that place. Goodbye! For all eternity! Goodbye, Mother Victoria! Forever and ever!

(Brigit throws in more dust and twists brush in a circular fashion. Rhythm of polishing/sweeping, singing and Mandy's dancing grows still faster.)

Brigit: Ha! Ha! John-Joe! Is it not hot enough for ya?
No? Purgatory isn't hot enough for my John-Joe! Oh! You're thirsty? You're all thirsty down there? All we have here is dirty

water! No! We've no porter or whiskey!
Look, Cathy, Mandy, Nellie-Nora! They're
all thirsty! Richard, John-Joe, His Lordship,
your fella, Cathy! And Elvis!

(Activity stops suddenly. Pause.)

Brigit: They're all burnin' with thirst!

*(Sudden full **sound** of washing-machines as women exit with brushes, polishers and return to set up for **Red Hearts Scene**.)*

Act 2 Scene 3

RED HEARTS

Brigit and Mandy move large laundry basket to position a little to right of centre and at a slight angle. Basket contains bundles of unwashed linens. Nellie-Nora sews at table centre left. Juliet to right of Nellie-Nora. Sewing-basket containing pin-cushion, needles and threads on table.

Mandy: Where's this basket from, Brigit?

Brigit: Athlone – you know – all around there! The middle of Ireland! Come on, Nellie-Nora! Juliet, help us with these filthy yokes! They're even worse than last week!

(Juliet moves to right of Brigit and Mandy at basket. Mandy examines label on unseen side of basket.)

Mandy: Do you not see the label, Brigit? This basket is not from Athlone! It's from Galway! From the City!

Juliet: From Galway? The City? But, this is a terrible job! Smellier than in the orphanage!

Cathy: Whites in this corner, Juliet! Coloureds over there! Socks in the middle!

Nellie-Nora: Search for cigarette-butts, Juliet! Don't forget trouser pockets! Mother o'God! Where did I put that last butt? – A match, Mandy! Quick!

Mandy: They're on the table, Nellie-Nora!

Juliet: Does Nellie-Nora smoke other people's cigarettes, Mandy?

Mandy: Yes! All the time, Juliet!

(Nellie-Nora finds a butt and matches. She lights butt. She keeps butt between her lips as she speaks. The others continue to sort dirty linens.)

Nellie-Nora: MMmn! That's better! Doesn't this lot come from your place, Cathy? Near the sea – ?

Cathy: Yes! Near the sea and the river. Though I can't smell salty seaweed!

(Turns her nose away.)

Juliet: Uuuch! Aah!

Brigit: I won't tell you what I smell! Do they ever wash themselves, Cathy?

Mandy: Would you look! *(Holds up white underpants covered with red hearts.)* From your place, Cathy? Look!

(Brigit grabs underpants and reads.)

Brigit: Made in the U. S. A.! Wouldn't you know! This fella doesn't wear his heart on his sleeve! He wears it on his Micky!

(Throws underpants in the air.)

Juliet: Oh no, Brigit! No! *(Dodges underpants.)*

Nellie-Nora: They're all below the waist!

Mandy: A smasher I'd say – a filmstar or an actor or – what do you think, Cathy?

(Mandy throws underpants to Brigit, who throws to Cathy and so on.)

Nellie-Nora: It's like what the Yanks would wear, Cathy!

Cathy: Yes! They wear funny clothes. Plaids, spots, stripes all mixed up together! I remember when the Yanks came home, when the second cousins from Boston visited! The colours they wore on the street!

Juliet: But – I thought you were off a farm, Cathy!

Nellie-Nora: No, Juliet! Cathy is from the city!

Cathy: *(dreamily)* A small city, Juliet! It's a lovely place –

(Cathy takes a man's silk dressing gown from basket, touches it lovingly.)

Mandy: A silk coat, Cathy? No! It's a dressing gown.

(Mandy touches the silk. Cathy is in a dream.)

Juliet: Why did you leave?

Nellie-Nora: She just couldn't stay, Juliet!

Mandy: The fellas – what were they like, Cathy?

Brigit: What're fellas always like? A few quick ones in a pub, then crowded like jack-daws at the door of a dance-hall, their minds as dirty as their fingernails!

Juliet: But Sister Virginia says only a few men are like that!

Brigit: Sister Virginia says! What does she know about it? Sqeezing through the dance-hall door was awful! When you'd be in the crush, some big hand would come out and grab you!

(Cathy puts dressing gown aside carefully.)

Cathy: I didn't go to dances much!

Nellie-Nora: They were terrible at the back of the chapel and in the organ-gallery! They were all the same!

Brigit: And they think we're the dirty ones!

Juliet: A dance! I never went to a dance! I think I'd like to go to one!

Brigit: Our Canon stood at the back of the dance-hall and watched! On Sundays he'd shout, "Company-keeping is a Mortal Sin! Hell for all Eternity!" When Ellen Moran got pregnant, he walked up and down outside her house in broad daylight saying the Rosary!

Nellie-Nora: A curse will fall on you, Brigit! Talking like that about the Canon!

(Mandy and Nellie-Nora bless themselves.)

Brigit: A curse! Don't be daft! I'm here – isn't that

enough? – The Canon's housekeeper bossed everyone in the parish! Bossed him too! Listened to all the gossip and gave the orders, pointing at us with her scarlet fingernails!

Nellie-Nora: I often think about Our Lady the time she got pregnant! Did the neighbours point at her too?

(Women smile.)

Nellie-Nora: She must have had a terrible time, when she began to show!

Mandy: But she had Saint Joseph! Didn't he stay with her!

Nellie-Nora: I wonder did the neighbours whisper and sneer?

Brigit: Gossiping neighbours going home from Mass like holy-water hens! Bloody hypocrites! But the missioners were the worst! Hellfire and brimstone every morning and evening!

Juliet: The dances, Mandy! Tell me!

Mandy: Well, Juliet! My second cousin, Jamsie loved women, but was afraid of courtin'. Halfway through the last dance, he'd say to his partner, – "I've to go now! Early start to-morrow! I've to drive my mother to teach in the Tech." He had no car of course! No mother either! All that fella had was an old crock of a bike! Poor Jamsie!

Cathy: In our city we had a glamour-boy, who did great business with tourists. He arranged with the ballroom porter to announce, "Dr. O'Connell is wanted urgently on the telephone! Dr. O'Connell! Dr. O'Connell!", while he was dancing cheek to cheek with some gorgeous blonde! "Excuse me, my love", he'd whisper. "One of my patients is very ill. I must check! I'll be back! Wait for me!" Success! The "doctor" bit never failed! They'd be waiting for him, when he came back after his pint in a pub down the road! Believing every word!

Brigit: Johnnie in Cillnamona! Mirrors on the tops of his dancing shoes!

Juliet: Mirrors on his dancing shoes? But why, Brigit?

(Brigit comes forward, calls Juliet and demonstrates Johnnie's antics.)

Brigit: You see, Juliet! When Johnnie was dancing with a girl, he...

Nellie-Nora: No! No, Brigit! Don't look at her, Juliet!

(Brigit dances and sings.)

Brigit: "Oh, Johnnie! Oh, Johnnie! Heavens above! Oh, Johnnie! Oh, Johnnie! How you can love!"

(A bell rings. A door bangs.)

Juliet: Shh! She's coming!

(Nellie-Nora goes to exit and listens to bell. Bn Bn. – Bn Bn.)

Nellie-Nora: That's Sister Virginia's bell! Mother Victoria's gone to his Lordship's Palace!

Brigit: Virginia! That piece of plaster!

Cathy: Aah, Brigit! I often wonder, why Sister Virginia wants to be a nun!

Brigit: She's probably afraid of men! Thinks it's easier to hide in here! But watch her! Soon she'll be strutting around like the others, waving her leather belt and treating us like dirt!

Nellie-Nora: No, Brigit! You're too hard on her!

Cathy: But she doesn't have to stay in here! She's

	not afraid of men, Brigit! Priests and seminarians come to visit her!
Nellie-Nora:	She can leave anytime she wants!
Brigit:	Sounds daft to me, Cathy! Staying in this dungeon with that cage on her head! How can she think straight?
Juliet:	I think I'd like to be a nun!
Cathy:	Well, you can't go to dances if you're a nun, Juliet!
Nellie-Nora:	I think you'd make a lovely nun!
Brigit:	Sure, they wouldn't have Juliet! Her mother was one of us!

(Stunned silence, as they continue to sort dirty clothes.)

Juliet:	Another cigarette-butt, Nellie-Nora! Look! Oh no! It's not! Look what I found!
Mandy:	Show me! Ooh! It's lipstick! Ooh! Lipstick!
Brigit:	In a trouser pocket!
Mandy:	Look! "Outdoor Girl"! – Rose Red – Mmmn! Where's the mirror, Nellie-Nora?
Nellie-Nora:	Here, Mandy!
Mandy:	Will you get the mirror, Juliet!

(Juliet takes mirror, gives it to Mandy. Mandy pouts as she puts on lipstick. Brigit takes lipstick and puts two spots, (rouge) on Mandy. Mandy decorates Brigit. They laugh and joke. Cathy and Juliet crowd around them. Brigit looks in mirror.)

Brigit:	Ach! Look at the cut o' me! You're like an Indian, Mandy! Rub it in! Like this!

(Mandy and Brigit rub one another's cheeks.
They laugh, but Nellie-Nora remains detached.)

Mandy:	Mmn! It tastes nice and perfumy! – How do I look?
Cathy:	You're gorgeous, Mandy! If only Elvis could see you now!

(Mandy prints her lips on hands.)

Brigit:	Now I'll paint you, Cathy.

Cathy: Can I do it myself, Brigit? Please?
(Brigit gives Cathy lipstick. Cathy paints her lips.)
Juliet: Will you put some on me, Cathy?
Cathy: Of course, Juliet! Stand here!
(Cathy paints Juliet's lips.)
Brigit: It suits your eyes, Juliet!
Juliet: My eyes?
Mandy: Don't heed her, Juliet!
(Brigit takes lipstick from Cathy and moves towards Nellie-Nora.)
Brigit: Come on, Nellie-Nora! A bit o' war-paint
                    for you! It'll cheer you up!
Nellie-Nora: No! Oh no!
(Brigit insists.)
Nellie-Nora   Noooo! Not lipstick!
(Nellie-Nora screams, wipes her lips and backs away. Brigit is upset. The others stare. Nellie-Nora is very agitated. Pause.)
Nellie-Nora: He – He – made me wear lipstick – and
                    perfume. He – wanted me to be like a city
                    girl. – No! No! He – He – in the room –
                    No! No, Mr. Persse! No! – Before he – he
                    hurt me! He wet me! No! No!
(Nellie-Nora takes sewing-basket from table and throws it to floor.)
Nellie-Nora: It's all your fault! All your fault!
(Nellie-Nora falls to floor. She hugs her knees then starts to rock her body. Sister Virginia enters carrying a box of Black Magic chocolates. She rushes to assist Nellie-Nora.)
Sister Virginia:
                    Now, what have you done, Brigit?
Brigit: Nothing, Sister!
Juliet: It's only lipstick, Sister!
Mandy: Rose Red lipstick. A bit o' colour, Sister!
Brigit: It's this place! This dungeon! This cage! And
                    you, Sister! Locking us up with your two

sets o' keys!

Sister Virginia:

I've chocolates here, Nellie-Nora! Take some!

Nellie-Nora: Get away from me!

Sister Virginia:

Here, Cathy! Mandy! Chocolates! Juliet?

(The women refuse chocolates.)

Brigit: Chocolates! Hhh! Keep your bloody chocolates. The keys, Pasty Face! Give me the keys!

Sister Virginia:

I – I can't! You know I can't give you the keys, Brigit!

Brigit: *(imitating Sister)* "You know I can't give you the keys, Brigit! I'll pray for you, Brigit!"

(Brigit blocks escape route.)

Brigit: Pretending to help! You're just like the rest o' them! You think if you keep us locked up, that we'll forget about living! About being alive! Don't you? That our heads will go soft and mushy from hymns and prayers! You think that we won't see what your crowd is up to! Well, Pasty Face! Brigit Murphy here sees through you! Sees through the whole lot o' you! Mother Superiors, Bishops, Popes and all!

(Sister Virginia fingers her Rosary Beads. Brigit approaches her.)

Brigit: Look at yourself, Pasty Face! You're a woman – Aren't you? Did you ever have a lover? Tell us that now, Sister! Ha? – Would you like a bit o' lipstick, Sister?

(Brigit holds lipstick menacingly. The women move away. Sister Virginia tries to escape, but Brigit pins her against wall.)

73

Brigit: You don't know anything! Never had a
lover! Never had a baby! So you're white
and shining, Sister! Not the same as us, are
you? Whose side are you on anyways? Why
aren't our lover-boys locked up too? One
law for them and another for us! Scab! Spy!
I'll daub it on the walls of Hell!

*(Brigit scribbles "Scab" on wall with lipstick, as she struggles with
Sister Virginia. She drags off Sister Virginia's veil and shouts)*

Brigit: I'll daub it on your baldy skull! Scab! Spy!
Informer!

*(She throws Sister Virginia to floor. Sister Virginia falls on
top of soiled linens. Juliet sits on floor and bites her nails.
Mandy hides behind basket. Nellie-Nora sobs and rocks her
body.)*

Brigit: *(change of tone)* All sweet smiles and
"Here's chocolates"! But you're as bad as the
rest! You're young and you keep the keys!
Stiff and starched you go back every night to
your nice white bed in your nice white cell!
You say your nice sweet prayers to your
Nice Clean God! Prayers and Hymns and
heaven when we die! No! No! No! Now is
what matters! We're alive now! It's no use
when we're dead! We want to live now!

Sister Virginia:

But I want to help, Brigit! I am on your side!

Brigit: No! You're not! I'd kill you, but you're not
worth it!

*(Brigit throws lipstick at Sister Virginia, takes box of chocolates
and throws contents on top of Sister Virginia. She moves towards
basket. Sister Virginia gets up slowly, tries to smooth her habit,
then, with dignity, walks through exit. Her white coif/veil is on
floor downstage. Brigit stands at basket.)*

Brigit: Rosa! Rosa! *(Second 'Rosa' a keening scream. Pause. Mandy peeps out from behind basket, finds scattered chocolates, eats one and puts some in pocket of her apron.)*

Mandy: She'll tell Mother Victoria on us!

Cathy: No. She mightn't tell. Sister Virginia mightn't! But we'll have to clean up the wall. Quick, Mandy! Get a bucket of hot water and a bottle of bleach. Hurry, Mandy!

(Mandy exits. Cathy tries to clean off lipstick from wall. Brigit hurriedly throws some clothes from basket. Visual rhythm of clothes thrown high in the air.)

Brigit: I'm going out now! In the basket! Come on! Quick! Help me!

(Cathy turns as Brigit speaks. Mandy returns with bucket.)

Mandy: I put half a bottle of bleach in, Cathy.

(Brigit steps into basket and kneels as she tries to cover herself with clothes.)

Brigit: I'm goin' out now to find my baby, Rosa. Cover me with clothes and push me into despatch! Quick! Stop staring at me! Help me!

(Cathy moves to Brigit.)

Cathy: But, Brigit! I wanted to! Please, Brigit, let me come with you! I'm so long trying!

Brigit: No! I'm going to find my Rosa!

Cathy: My twins, Brigit! Please!

Brigit: *(screams)* No! I'm going alone now!

Cathy: *(screams)* My Emily! My Michele!

(Brigit tries to close basket. Cathy is hyper-ventilating. Mother Victoria enters, looks at writing on wall and walks around slowly as she speaks)

Mother Victoria:

What's all this about? Get out of that basket, Brigit! Stand up, Nellie-Nora! Stop that snivelling, Cathy McNamara! Back to work immediately, Mandy! You too, Juliet! – Where's Sister Virginia? Why isn't she here? Why?

(Brigit steps out of basket. The others obey automatically. As Mother Victoria exits, she sees Sister Virginia's veil/coif on floor. She picks it up. The stiffly starched empty veil/coif held on high by Mother Victoria looks like a head-trophy. She turns to Brigit.)

Mother Victoria:

What's this, Brigit? This? – To my office immediately, Brigit Murphy! His Lordship will hear about you!

Brigit: No! No! I'm not going!

Mother Victoria:

(shouts) To my office now, Brigit Murphy!

(Brigit walks reluctantly in front of Mother Victoria towards exit.)

Mother Victoria:

I always knew you were an evil woman!

(Cathy gets idea of going out alone in basket. She waits until Mother Victoria has gone.)

Cathy: *(excitedly)* I can go now! Me! Help me, Mandy! Please, Nellie-Nora!

(Cathy steps into basket. Nellie-Nora moves to help her.)

Cathy: Cover me! Will you help me, Juliet? Hurry! Hurry!

Nellie-Nora: Are you sure, Cathy? Are you alright?

(They cover Cathy with bundles of clothes. Nellie-Nora places a purple drape on top)

Cathy: Hurry! Please! Hurry! The van will be gone!

Mandy: We'll be thinking of you, Cathy!

(They close basket. Nellie-Nora opens basket to say)

Nellie-Nora: Have you that Holy Medal I gave you?

Cathy: Hurry! Hurry!

(They close basket, fasten metal locks and push it hurriedly through exit.)
Lights *lower.*
(Pause. Mandy, Brigit and Nellie-Nora return to set up for Act 2 Scene 4 Office 2)

Sound up for Plain Chant *Magnificat* sung by one soprano voice.

Act 2 Scene 4

OFFICE 2

Set as in Office 1 may be used, but a small table with telephone a little to left of centre is sufficient. Lights down except for highlight on Mother Victoria, who is standing centre stage. She taps her office-book with crucifix.

Sound: *Plain Chant "Magnificat" sung by one soprano voice as in Act 2 Scene 1. Plain Chant fades as Sister Virginia stands at 'door of office.'*

Mother Victoria:
>Come in!

(Sister Virginia enters, pauses.)

Mother Victoria:
>What delayed you, Sister? – On your knees!

(Sister Virginia hesitates.)

Mother Victoria:
>On your knees, Sister!

(Sister Virgina kneels, head bowed, then looks straight at Mother Victoria.)

Mother Victoria:
>I told you to keep aloof from those women!
>I warned you about Brigit Murphy!

Sister Virginia:
>But they are our Sisters in Christ, Mother Victoria!

Mother Victoria:
>Our Sisters!

Sister Virginia:

>Yes, Mother Victoria! Part of His Mystical
Body!

Mother Victoria:

>You are lucky you are not scarred for life!

Sister Virginia:

>We are scarred! We, their jailers!

Mother Victoria:

>Scarred! You disobeyed me again, Sister!

(Takes open letter from office-book and pushes it towards Sister Virginia.)

Mother Victoria:

>This letter! Sealed without my permission!

(Pause.)

Sister Virginia:

>Yes, Mother Victoria! His Lordship should
come to this laundry! He should see things
as they really are!

Mother Victoria:

>His Lordship, the Bishop, in that laundry
talking to – those – those – sinful women!

Sister Virginia:

>Yes, Mother Victoria!

(Sister Virginia stands.)

Mother Victoria:

>On your knees, Sister!

(Sister Virginia kneels.)

Mother Victoria:

>*(reads letter)* "My Lord Bishop, as you are
patron of this laundry, I invite you to visit
us at our workplace. You should see and
speak to the mothers, who are locked in
here. Out of the goodness of your heart,
you will, I am sure, allow them weekly
visits to the orphanage. Their conditions of

work and diet need to be improved
immediately. Because of the deterioration in
the health of a woman called Cathy
McNamara, I beg you to come before you
leave for Rome. I am, my Lord, your
obedient and humble servant Sister Virginia
O'Brien."

(Pause.)
Mother Victoria:

Why didn't you give me this letter before
you sealed it? Why?

(Sister stands.)
Mother Victoria:

On your knees!

(Pause. Sister kneels.)
Sister Virginia:

You'd quote Rules, Mother Victoria! You'd -

Mother Victoria:

(interrupts) During my thirty years in this
community, I've never come across such –
such impudence! A white novice takes it on
herself to invite that holy man to visit those–
those – !

(She crumples letter and throws it to floor.)
Sister Virginia:

Permission to say more, Mother Victoria?

Mother Victoria:

More to say, Sister Virginia? Is that
seminarian putting ideas into your head?

Sister Virginia:

I can think for myself, Mother Victoria!

*(Telephone rings. Mother Victoria answers as she points her
hand to silence Sister Virginia.)*
Mother Victoria:

(softly) Hellooouuu! Yeees! *(sharper tone)*

Oh, Sister Perpetuo! — Ring the Mass Bell
now! – And breakfast for that missionary
priest in the small parlour! Tea and toast will
do him!

(Mother Victoria bangs down telephone.)
Sister Virginia:

Maybe I should write to His Holiness!
Mother Victoria:

Did you say something, Sister Virginia?
(A Mass bell rings.)
Sister Virginia:

I must write to His Holiness! It takes a long
time for news of change to reach this island,
this laundry!

(Pause. Mother Victoria straightens her back.)
Mother Victoria:

Now I have something to say to you, Sister
Virginia O'Brien! Your brother, Father John, is
saying Mass in the side-chapel!
(Sister Virginia stands up.) On your knees,
Sister! *(Slowly Sister kneels.)* He has asked
for you from the Altar! Imagine! From God's
Holy Altar!

Sister Virginia:

Permission, please, to serve my brother's
Mass!
Mother Victoria:

No! You may not serve his Mass! No! You
may not speak to him afterwards!
Sister Virginia:

But I must see my brother! I must speak to
him!
Mother Victoria:

No, Sister! You may not see him!
Sister Virginia:

I must speak to him! I must! I must speak

Mother Victoria:

> Back to the laundry! Now! Remember
> Blind Obedience, Sister Virginia O'Brien!
> Blind Obedience!

(Sister Virginia rises from her knees and leaves office. Pause. Mother Victoria picks up crumpled letter, looks at it and says)

Mother Victoria:

> A white novice says, she'll write to His
> Holiness! – *(puzzled and worried).* My Lord
> Bishop, what is happening to our Holy
> Church?

*(Mother Victoria turns and leaves office. **Lights** change.)*

Sound: Plain Chant *Magnificat* as women set up for **Act 2 Scene 5, Discovery.**

Act 2 Scene 5

DISCOVERY

Afternoon of next day. Same workroom set. Nellie-Nora and Mandy sew at table centre left. Laundry basket up right. Brigit scrubs at wash-board centre right. Folded sheets and blankets on shelves.

Sound: *Low hum of washing-machines.*

Nellie-Nora: Such a hullabaloo last night! Aach! Must be a lot o' sore heads this morning!

Mandy: I couldn't sleep!

Nellie-Nora: One fella kept shoutin', "Goodnight, Reverend Mother! Sweet dreams, Reverend Mother! Sleep tight! Don't let the fleas bite, Reverend Mother!"

Brigit: I wonder if the fellas from Cillnamona were up! Dark suits over farmer tans! Pioneer pins pushed under lapels, foolin' their mothers!

Mandy: I heard the drums and the saxophones. But why didn't they play Elvis's music?

(Mandy breaks down in tears.)

Nellie-Nora: I couldn't sleep either, wonderin' about Cathy! Aach, don't cry, Mandy! What's the use? There's broken hearts out there too! Elvis'll send you another photo! He'll write to you! He will!

(Nellie-Nora gives Mandy her Elvis scrapbook.)

Mandy: *(change of tone)* No! He won't! I know he won't! *(Mandy throws scrapbook onto floor.)*

My only chance is to do what Cathy did!
Would she be there now?

Nellie-Nora: She should be! Mother o'God, she should!

(Nellie-Nora picks up scrapbook and puts it on table near Mandy. Mandy pushes it away.)

Brigit: Mother Victoria can't drag her back this time! The Black Viper threatened the Big House on me! She's the one that should be in there! Power mad! Money mad! More money-for-the-Bishop mad!

Mandy: Puttin' poor Juliet back in the orphanage!

Brigit: The rip says we're bad company for a young girl! – Ugh! They're all the same! Virginia! Victoria!

Nellie-Nora: Poor Sister Virgina! She didn't tell!

Mandy: Yes, Brigit! She didn't tell on us!

Brigit: Hasn't she two eyes? Two ears? Can't she see what's going on?

(Enter Sister Virginia carrying broken sunflowers. Daisy-like flowers if sunflowers not available. She notices Mandy's distress.)

Sister Virginia:

Put these in water, Mandy. Please.

Brigit: Flowers here? Flowers from the sun? No, Sister! Keys!

(Mandy takes flowers and proceeds to pull petals away one by one as she says.)

Mandy: "He loves me! He loves me not. He loves me. He loves me not."

(Mandy repeats this chant as she tears flowers and stalks into fragments, throws them on floor and stamps on them, picks them up and tears them apart.)

Sister Virginia:

Where's Cathy? – Is she in the steam-room?

(Sister Virginia looks into side-rooms and returns.)

Sister Virginia:

Have you seen her, Mandy?

Nellie-Nora: No, Sister!

Sister Virginia:

Brigit?

(No response from Brigit.)

Sister Virginia:

When did you see her last?

Nellie-Nora: Last night, Sister!

Sister Virginia:

Not since last night? Why didn't somebody tell me?

(She moves towards cloister.)

Nellie-Nora: But sure, you were in the kitchen all mornin', Sister! How could we?

(Sister Virginia notices blankets on shelf.)

Sister Virginia:

Those blankets should have gone in the Athlone basket! Will you parcel them, Brigit? Put a label on them?

(No response from Brigit.)

Sister Virginia:I'll do it myself! – Maybe Cathy is sick! Where could she be? – Maybe – I must speak to Mother Victoria!

(A bell tolls. Keys rattle. Mother Victoria enters, walks slowly to Sister Virginia and whispers. She offers overall to Sister Virginia, who refuses to take it. The women pretend to work. Mother Victoria turns to women, puts apron on table and moves down centre.)

Mother Victoria:

I – I – We must all pray now. We must pray for Cathy!

Brigit: She got to Galway? She did?

Nellie-Nora: What's wrong, Mother?

Mandy: Did she get the twins? Tell us, Mother!

Sister Virginia:
In the basket! May she rest in peace!

Brigit: Rest in peace? Cathy? No! No!

Mandy: Cathy? She got out! She's outside! She got to Galway!

Sister Virginia:
They found her in the basket! Her asthma!

Nellie-Nora: It's a mistake, Sister! It's not our Cathy! No! No!

Mother Victoria:
We must pray!

(Sister Virginia confronts Mother Victoria.)

Sister Virginia:
Her asthma, Mother! Cathy suffocated! I told you she needed attention! Her attacks were ...

Mother Victoria:
It was an accidental death! We must pray for her soul! The first sorrowful mystery, The Agony in the Garden. Our Father who art in heaven. Hallowed be Thy name. Thy Kingdom come. Thy will be done on earth.

(Brigit and Nellie-Nora walk around in a confused state. Nellie-Nora calls out Cathy's name. Mandy, kneeling and holding broken flowers, moves from Mother Victoria to Sister Virginia.)

Brigit: I should have gone! I was goin' first! I wouldn't have suffocated!

Nellie-Nora: No! No, Brigit! I should've stopped her! – No! It's a mistake! It's somebody else! It's not our Cathy!

Mother Victoria:
Thy will be done on earth as it is in Heaven. Give us this day our daily bread and *(small bell rings)* forgive us our

trespasses as we forgive those who trespass against us. And lead us not into temptation but deliver us from evil. Finish the prayers, Sister Virginia! My bell calls.

Nellie-Nora: Amen!

Sister Virginia:

Yes, Mother Victoria. Hail Mary full of grace! The Lord is with Thee. Blessed art Thou amongst women and blessed is the fruit of Thy womb, Jesus.

(Mandy and Nellie-Nora sob and contradict one another. Brigit moves and stands menacingly behind Sister Virginia.)

Brigit: The keys, Sister! You'll give us the keys! We'll get out now! Won't we, Sister?

Sister Virginia:

Pray, Brigit! We must pray for Cathy! Hail, Mary full of grace. The Lord is with thee. Blessed art Thou amongst women and blessed is the fruit of Thy womb, Jesus!

(Sister Virginia turns to face Brigit. They stare at one another. Pause. Sister Virginia unclips keys from her belt and praying "Holy Mary, Mother of God" etc, gives keys to Brigit. Brigit grabs them.)

Brigit: Ye're the ones that are dead, Virginia! Dead inside yer laundry basket hearts!

(Shouts as she runs through audience and away.)

Brigit: Yer laundry basket hearts!

(Sister Virginia, praying softly, moves upstage to wall. Mandy prays "Hail Mary" and "Holy Mary Mother of God pray for us sinners now and at the hour of our death" continuously, distractedly, as she washes clothing in basin.)

Lights *lower.*

Sound: *Voice of Kathleen Ferrier*

"He was despised. Despised and rejected. Rejected of men.

A man of sorrows.
A man of sorrows
And acquainted with grief."

(as Nellie-Nora in Slow Movement takes purple drapes from shelves and covers/shrouds Mandy, Sister Virginia and table. She puts Cathy's apron into basket and moves it down left. (Same position as in Act 1 Scene 1.) She slowly looks around laundry space and exits.)

Sound up of *He was despised.*

Straight into **Epilogue, Act 2 Scene 6**)

Epilogue

ACT 2 SCENE 6

Time: 1992

Lights: Low after Discovery Scene.

Sound: Voice of Kathleen Ferrier
                    "He was despised.
                    Despised and rejected.
                    Rejected of men.
                    A man of sorrows.
                    A man of sorrows
                    And acquainted with grief."
                    from Handel's "Messiah".

*Set as in Act 1 Scene 1 but drapes are not hanging. Rosa,
carrying Laundry Register and Black Magic box, enters and
moves downstage to laundry basket. Mandy and Sister
Virginia shrouded-frozen in purple drapes. Highlight comes
up on basket.*
Sound: *Music fades as Nellie-Nora (aged) shuffles on. Dragged-
slipper sound.*

Nellie-Nora: Did you find what you were looking for,
                    Rosa?
Rosa: Brigit Murphy and a girl, Rosa?
Nellie-Nora: Yes!
Rosa: And this photograph, "My baby, Rosa". Is
                    this me?

*(Rosa shows photograph to Nellie-Nora. Nellie-Nora
examines it.)*

Nellie-Nora: Ah Rosa, that's just a photograph she found
                    in an unwashed pocket! Brigit adopted that
                    paper-baby. She let on it was you!
Rosa: So – It's not – me. A paper-baby? She called

90

	me Rosa! Everyone calls me Caroline! – But why, Nellie-Nora, why did she ever come here?
Nellie-Nora:	Brigit was put in here! Her brother signed her in before he got married! When Cathy died, she disappeared. Not a word, not a trace of her since!
Rosa:	Where did she go?
Nellie-Nora:	I don't know, Rosa! Maybe she went back to Cillnamona – to try to see John-Joe!
Rosa:	John-Joe? Is he my father? Do you know his last name, his address?
Nellie-Nora:	No, Rosa! She only ever called him, John-Joe! He must live near Cillnamona!
Rosa:	Do you think he's still there? Do you think she's alive?
Nellie-Nora:	I don't know, Rosa.
Rosa:	Would you have heard if –
Nellie-Nora:	I don't know! After Saint Paul's closed that time, none of the women ever came back to visit. I suppose they wanted to forget this place.
Rosa:	I must go to Cillnamona to-morrow!

(Rosa moves nearer to Nellie-Nora)

Rosa:	Did Brigit talk about – going – to look for me?
Nellie-Nora:	She always wanted to find you, Rosa! It broke her heart giving you up like that. You can be certain she tried! You can be certain she spent the rest of her life lookin' for you!
Rosa:	Can I take these? *(Black Magic Box with photographs and ledger.)* Would anybody mind? And the paper-baby too?
Nellie-Nora:	Yes, Rosa! I don't think anyone knows they're still here.

(Rosa moves closer to Nellie-Nora.)

Rosa: Maybe I'll call to see you again, – if that's alright?

Nellie-Nora: Yes, Rosa! That'd be nice.

Rosa: Would you like to visit us at Shannon, Nellie-Nora? I'll collect you myself in the car?

Nellie-Nora: *(shaking)* No! No, Rosa! I – I – I don't go out much.

*(Nellie-Nora, head shaking and hand in tremor, turns away and crumples towards basket. Rosa looks at her for a moment, then hurries away into audience. Nellie-Nora suddenly looks out towards Rosa, then takes a long look at the old laundry workspace. As **sound** of Kathleen Ferrier's voice comes up*

"Despised, rejected.

Rejected of men.

A man of sorrows.

A man of sorrows

And acquainted with grief."

*(Nellie-Nora shuffles dragged-slipper-**sound** to light-switch on wall. As she switches off light, fade music, lower lights.*
Sound*: Voice over: (Sister Virginia)*

In 1992, to make place for a building development at St. Paul's Home, the remains of Mary Kate Dempsey, Mary Jane O'Sullivan, Kitty O'Hara, Julia Mannion, Betty and Annie Gormley, Ellen McAuley, Cathy McNamara and three hundred other unnamed penitents were exhumed, cremated and reburied outside in Killmacha Cemetery. Mandy Prenderville has not left the local Mental Institution since 1963.

END

Music in *Eclipsed*

CLASSICAL
Contralto Aria *He was despised* from Handel's Oratorio *Messiah* sung by Kathleen Ferrier.
(Orchestral introduction and Aria for opening and closing scenes.)

PLAIN CHANT
One Soprano voice sings the *Magnificat.*
One Soprano voice sings the *Credo* from *Missa de Angelis.*

ROCK AND ROLL SONGS OF ELVIS PRESLEY
Heartbreak Hotel
It's now or never!
Have I told you lately that I love you?

OTHER TUNES
Daisy, Daisy, Give me your answer. Do!
True Love
Oh, Johnnie! Oh, Johnnie! Heavens above! (Two lines)
The Bells of the Angelus/On Top of Old Smokey (Brigit uses Bells of the Angelus melody for On Top of Old Smokey)
In Act 2 Floor Scene 2 (Floor) the women hum melody of *The Irish Washerwoman.* Cathy uses tabletop or washboard as bodhrán percussion.
Women hum melody of plain chant *Magnificat* above machine sounds for scene changes.

About the Playwright

PATRICIA BURKE BROGAN is a painter, poet and playwright. Her etchings have won awards at Barcelona and at Listowel International Biennale 1982. Her collection of poetry, *Above The Waves Calligraphy* and the script of her stage play, *Eclipsed*, were published by Salmon Publishing in 1994. The script of her stage play, *Stained Glass At Samhain*, a companion piece to *Eclipsed*,was published in 2002.

Eclipsed has won many awards including a Fringe First at Edinburgh Theatre Festival 1992 and the USA Moss Hart Award 1994.

Stained Glass at Samhain and *Eclipsed* have been translated into Italian. *Eclipsed* has also been translated into French, Dutch, Japanese, Spanish and Irish.

Eclipsed has been excerpted in documentaries and other collected works including *The Field Day Anthology of Irish Writing, Volumes 4 and 5. Irish Women Playwrights of the Twentieth Century. Ireland's Women: Writings Past and Present. Motherhood in Ireland. Repositories of Secrecy and Shame; Magdalene Laundries and Ireland's Architecture of Containment. Sacred Play: Soul Journeys in Contemporary Irish Theatre: Druids, Dudes and Beauty Queens:The Changing Face of Irish Theatre. Laundry Basket Hearts: Visions and Revisions of the Magdalene Laundries in the Drama of Patricia Burke Brogan. Theatre Journal 1991. I Magdalene Laundries Nelle Opere Di Patricia Burke Brogan (Verona). Il Concetto Di Dignita Nella Cultura Occidentale (Urbino) The Concept of Dignity in Western Culture. The Power of Visual Elements in Patricia Burke Brogan's Work (University of Delaware)* and in *Amnesty International Magazine 2002.*

Clarenda's Mirror, a three-act play, was chosen by the artistic panel of the 4th International Women Playwrights Conference for the Irish Showcase at the Galway Conference in June 1997.

Requiem Of Love, A Monologue for stage was published by Wordsonthe street in 2006 and launched at the Cúirt International Festival of Literature. Her poetry collection *Décollage: New and Selected Poems* was published by Wordsonthestreet in 2008.

Patricia received an Arts Council Bursary in Literature in 1993, a European Script Writers' Fund in 1994, and an Arts Council Bursary in Drama in 2005.

OTHER TITLES BY PATRICIA BURKE BROGAN
FROM WORDSONTHESTREET

Requiem of Love
A monologue for stage
ISBN 9780955260407
56 pp RRP €11.00 pb

Décollage
New and Selected Poems
ISBN 9780955260469
104pp RRP €12.00 pb

Memoir with Grykes & Turloughs

ISBN 9781907017292
300 pp RRP €18.00 pb Illustrated.

Stained Glass at Samhain
Continuing the story of Mother Victoria
ISBN 9781907017285
76 pp RRP €11.00 pb

Log on to our online bookshop at:
www.wordsonthestreet.com

Or order from:

Wordsonthestreet
Six San Antonio Park
Salthill
Galway Ireland
Email: publisher@wordsonthestreet.com

Lightning Source UK Ltd.
Milton Keynes UK
UKHW020818300620
365790UK00005B/191